WRITING MEMOIR
How to write a story from your life
SECOND EDITION

Anna Meryt

First published in December 2017
by Tambourine Press Ltd
5 Harringay Gdns, London, N8 0SE

Front Cover Designed by Freya Newmarch
Photos owned by Anna Meryt
Illustrations by Anna Meryt

WRITING MEMOIR

How to write a story from your life

SECOND EDITION

Anna Meryt

Tambourine
Press

There is no greater agony than bearing an untold story inside you.

Maya Angelou

Don't die with your music still in you.

Wayne Dyer

Hello to my readers,

Firstly, this is a new edition. I've updated the publishing section now, as Amazon changed it's publishing platform from CreateSpace to Kindle Direct Publishing (KDP).

This book was written to help and guide you through the process of telling your story. How do you write it all down in the best possible way so people will read it, from beginning to end?

In this book you'll discover

• Whether you really want to write a memoir?

• Perhaps you've already begun? Where do you go from here? How do you plan to reach the end?

• Or you haven't started yet, but something happened to you and you know it'll make an interesting story?

• Or a series of things happened to you that are unusual, shocking, historical or unique?

• You want some support and guidance to get you from start to finish? Throughout the book I give short exercises to get you practicing the key points in the chapter you've just read.

My Background

Firstly, you might want to know a bit about who I am. I've written and published one memoir and I'm half way through the second. I have based *this* book on what I learned from writing the first one, which was called ***A Hippopotamus at the Table*** and is set in 1970s South Africa. I'm sure, (had I spent more time) I could have improved it. But it's a good story, and it was time to let go and move on to the next project.

Throughout *this* book, I refer back to the first memoir and include extracts here and there. This is to illustrate the process I went through and also, telling anecdotes/stories about the author's process helps to bring a '*how to*' book to life. My second memoir will be called **Beyond the Bounds** and is set in London and Indonesia.

Teaching my memoir course participants taught me a great deal and their stories continually fascinated me. Then the various writing groups to which I have belonged and hearing their feedback have been invaluable for improving my writing too.

Before that, I had a varied career, going in all sorts of directions – teaching in Adult and Higher Education, delivering programmes to offenders in Criminal Justice and finally working with victims of violence for eleven years. Meanwhile, I was writing poetry and began to get poems published in anthologies and literary magazines. I had also started writing my first memoir **A Hippopotamus at the Table** and joined a writing group. I completed an MA in Professional Writing in 2010. In 2011, I won first prize in the Lupus International Poetry competition, then published two poetry collections **Heart Broke** (2013) and **Dolly Mix** (2014). **A Hippopotamus at the Table** was published in 2015.

I've travelled quite a bit in Africa – usually solo. I always take my small laptop with me and write as I go along – in cafes or libraries. I still do that in London. The British Library is my favourite place to write or sometimes, sitting in a beach café somewhere on the Mediterranean always inspires me.

***

If you enjoy this book and find it useful, can you kindly review it on Amazon? This is very important for keeping book sales steady and placing me in the Amazon rankings for this genre. Just give it a star rating and write one line – whatever you like – a variety of reviews is important.

TABLE OF CONTENTS

Chapter 1 What is memoir?

It's a big question, *what is memoir* and much discussed by writers, readers and the literati. Here's a working definition – ***it's a part of your life, not the whole life.***

A whole life is an autobiography.

'Autobiographies are favoured by nerds and children doing book reports. They are an account of everything that has ever happened to you in chronological order and they are boring.

Memoirs are more fun. Memoirs focus on selected moments from your life that hold great importance...'[1]

A memoir could cover two weeks, two months, two years or even five years of your life. Something happened to you, in your chosen period of time, that you want to write about - something different, possibly something dramatic, perhaps it changed your life in some way?

[1] Corinne Caputo, A Writer's Guide to Fame and Fortune

Memoir isn't the summary of a life. It's a window into a life. Very much like a photograph in its selective composition. It may look like a casual, even random calling up of bygone events. It's not. It's a deliberate construction.'[2]

As a memoir writer, I have often been told, 'Why don't you just tell your story as fiction – many writers do? You avoid lots of problems that way.' Many writers decide it's the only way to tell their story – they can anonymise it and change the story around and fictionalise the characters involved. That's one option.

But I've always liked to read memoirs, because I enjoy reading stories that are 'true'. Often they are breathtakingly extraordinary. When you've had something interesting, dramatic or unusual happen in your life, you want to tell the true story, put it on record. These stories are often better than fiction because you know they're real. You may feel (as I do), that you have a duty to tell some of your stories – if only as historical reference for those born after many of the events.

My first memoir - **A Hippopotamus at the Table** was set in 1970s South Africa, the apartheid era. What was it like to be there and observe that time as an outsider? Those who read my book will find that out.

What other reasons are there to write memoir not fiction? Writing my own memoir gave me an insight into the pitfalls and challenges of the genre. Those of us who write memoir have, I believe, a particular calling to

[2] On Writing Well, William Zinsser. (1990) Harper Collins.

write truth (as we see it) and NOT fiction. We're driven if you like.

I've been teaching memoir writing for a while, to small but enthusiastic groups, whose stories were diverse, fascinating and unique. I'd love to read each of those people's whole story in a book. I'm hoping, some of them at least, will get written.

How is writing for memoir different to writing fiction? Here's a quote from Professor Judith Barrington in her book 'Writing the Memoir':

'In memoir, the author stands behind [his or] her story saying to the world: this happened, this is true. What is important about this assertion is the effect on the reader – he [or she] reads it believing it to be remembered experience, which in turn requires the writer to be an unflinchingly reliable narrator. ...

In fiction ... if a writer presents it as fiction, the reader will usually perceive it as fiction. ... in memoir [the reader's perception is] the central commitment not to fictionalise.'

* * *

Your starting point is - what do you want to write about? Is it a particular event that happened to you? Something readers will connect with? When I asked my group what would make them pick up a memoir in a bookshop, here's what they said:

• a story about something that rings bells for them – a place, a time, an era that they recognise from their own past. It might be a story set in the 60s/70s/80s/90s/noughties. It might be a story where the writer mentions pop idols from their past, from their teenage years, dramatic events that they remember – wars, political upheavals, something in the news – all important to give context to the story.

• a story about a time or place they know very little about, but they'd like to know more for example, '**A Hippopotamus at the Table**', my book about living in South Africa in the time of apartheid, or The Girl With Seven Names by Heuonsu Lee about growing up in North Korea.

• Some write redemption stories – for example - *I went through this and survived and this is how,* like Angela's Ashes, by Frank McCourt.

• Some write revenge stories (for example, Constance Briscoe in 'Ugly.'). A member of my memoir class was writing a revenge story, about a work environment where she felt badly treated by an awful boss - she wrote with a great deal of humour, making the group laugh out loud.

• A woman on my course, was writing about travelling in Namibia for three months – a theme started to emerge of betrayal, loss of trust.

• A young woman had left school and travelled extensively in South East Asia – she'd kept a diary. She wanted to write a story for gap year students, so they'd know what it was like, from her experiences.

• Another woman was writing a book about growing up in a religious cult in America and escaping.

• Another was writing about being part of the crew on a round the world yacht race.

There are so many different themes, travel and adventure, redemption and revenge, religion and spirituality, war and survival, romantic and psychological, journeys both real and metaphorical - whatever your story is about I'd love to read it one day, if you write it well. Remember, each story (yours too) is unique.

The next question is, who are you writing for? Your Mum, Dad, your kids, friends, the wider public? Do you hope to be a best-selling author one day, or just produce a book for a small circulation? Do you have a story that you feel is so interesting and unusual that it would appeal to a wide audience?

After that consider what your writing skills are like? The skill of becoming a good writer must be learned through practise, like any other skill. Do your writing skills need to be improved by doing some creative writing courses, joining a writers' group and getting feedback?

Before we move on to planning your book, a few more things to consider. Often people have no idea of how to narrow down the scope of their memoir. Remember, you're not writing your whole life – that would be an autobiography. Here's an exercise to narrow down the focus of what you're writing about:

WRITING EXERCISE – Where to start?

So where and how are you going to begin your memoir? What is the starting point? Year? Month?

Usually I tell my students to go into a bookshop or library, pick up some books and read the first page – see what gets you hooked in, so you really want to read more and buy the book. I rewrote my first page many times. Remember, it's the window into the rest of your book, it's important. Also write something for now, nothing's fixed, you can change things around anytime.

Ready to write? Pick up a pen and an A4 pad and write

START.

My memoir will start in (year) …
It'll cover (how long?)
It'll end when ….

Set your timer on your alarm or phone for 10-15 minutes.

1. For example. I'll start my book in 1999 a week before the millennium. It'll cover those 6 months when I split up with my boyfriend and jumped on a plane for Kenya, with some mad idea to go visit my long lost uncle in Nairobi. Maybe it'll finish on the day when I came back to the UK 6 months later?
or …
2. One of my students decided to write about a *2 week* period in her life – it started on the day she was arrested in Los Angeles in 199?, because

her visa had run out. It ended when she was released and flew back to the UK. Her story covered the time from her arrest, being in the female prison, until her deportation.
or …

3. It happened when I was (age?). The story I want to tell, lasted for X months, X years. It changed me, had a profound effect on me because …

Just write for those ten-fifteen minutes. Everything you can think of around the events that started off the story – what characters were involved (yes name them, the names you know – this is just for you, we can think about name-changes later). Keep your pen down (or fingers on keyboard) for about half a page.

When the timer beeps, finish your sentence and re-read what you've written – preferably out loud if you're on your own – or to a friend.

Just remember this is your first idea. You can change the details or even all of it later. Now you have an idea where your story is going to start. Leave it (not too long) to marinade in your mind until you're ready to write more.

"One of the best gifts you have to offer when you write personal history is the gift of yourself. Don't forget it's there and it has great power. Give yourself permission to write about yourself, and have a good time doing it.'
On Writing Well by William Zinsser

Chapter 2 Truth is stranger than ...

Do memoir writers have to tell the whole truth, nothing but the truth? Is telling the truth even possible as a memoir writer? Remember that contract with the reader? But all truth is subjective isn't it? Let's think about that for a moment.

We all believe we're able to tell the truth, we know exactly what the truth is and it's relatively easy to tell the difference between what is true and what is not? Yes?

Here's a quote from a Buddhist leader of the Triratna Order - a worldwide Western Buddhist group. **Sangharakshita** is brilliant at analysing and drawing out the deepest meaning of certain concepts. Here's his analysis of truth telling.[3] *He* starts by saying

'We all think we know exactly what is meant when it is said that all speech should be truthful.'

He goes on to discuss truth in relation to factual accuracy. He breaks down truth telling

---

[3] Vision and Transformation. Sangharakshita. 1990 Windhorse Pubs.

into a variety of components of which factual accuracy is just one.

'We all tend to twist, distort or at least slightly bend facts, in the direction in which we would like them to go.' He talks about adding to factual accuracy an *'attitude of honesty and sincerity ... saying what you really think.'*

Easy yes? Until he asks whether most of us actually *'know what we think?'* and asserts *'Most of us live in a chronic state of mental confusion, bewilderment, chaos and disorder....how can we therefore speak the truth?'*

I regularly have people in my groups who say they're worried about whether they will remember enough. Will they be able to write with any accuracy of events that often happened a long time ago?

For my second memoir, I'm writing of events that happened 13 years ago (my first book was written about events from circa 35+ years ago.) Before I start writing a chapter, I have a vague idea of the general scenario as it happened. What comes out, as I begin to write, is several thousand words about, for example, visiting someone in a police cell in Indonesia, descriptive passages, details, conversations.

Out of the chaos and disorder in my head a coherent story appears. I can compare this to Steven King's description of his writing process - like an archaeologist with a trowel, scraping away the dirt to uncover a story. He is talking about characters and events emerging in his fiction writing.

This process, of clearing away the mud and stones in my memory, enables me to put remembered events into some kind of order, so that I can glue them together into a cohesive story. The first part of the process is thinking about what happened. The next part is putting pen to paper (or fingers to keyboard) and writing the first sentence.

Before you start writing, you think you can't remember much, and then by magic the words tumble out onto the page. The story emerges, sometimes slowly, painfully, sometimes coming to a dead halt. But then suddenly your fingers fly across the keyboard (or A4 pad). It's amazing what you remember when you start digging. When I focus in to a memory, I'm almost there, watching the events unfold again. You remember far more than you think, once you start writing.

My groups liked me calling the process 're-imagining'. This word seems to help them let go of a rigid idea of the memoir writing process – where truth-telling and factual accuracy *must* be adhered to at all costs. Just let the story flow through you. Truth is important, but the process should be relaxed and creative. How you present the story and your truth is unique and original to you.

What I'm writing about, is from my own subjective viewpoint. One of the other characters in my account might well remember it differently, with different angles and perspectives – that's their truth. I can only write about mine. You can only write about yours.

Don't worry about it, just write and see what emerges.

It's very gratifying when you send a chapter to someone who was there with you, (I have had experience of this), who says 'that's exactly how it happened'. But I've also had the experience of someone (who was present) saying

'Oh that didn't happen did it? You created it for dramatic effect.'

'NO I didn't, it really happened and you were there.'

'Well I don't remember that at all.'

Memory can be elusive as well as subjective. So can truth, but we have a duty as memoir writers to keep our focus on the truth, as near as we can.

* * *

'The core, ethical concepts in which you most passionately believe are the language in which you are writing.' … and …Your whole piece is the truth, not just one shining epigrammatic moment in it. There will need to be some kind of unfolding in order to contain it and there will need to be layers…. This is what may take a whole book.'[4]

'Because everyone knows and accepts that memoir is by nature partial and thematic, you can begin and end where you like and leave out what you like – though you cannot add and invent what you like!'[5]

[4] Bird By Bird. Anne Lamott (1994) Anchor Books
[5] The Arvon Book of Life Writing, Sally Cline and Carole Angier [p163] (2010) Methuen Drama

Exercise

Spend ten minutes writing about an event that you want to include in your memoir. Be immediate, as if you're watching it unfolding in front of you. Include the place, the scene, describe the setting. Sounds and colour bring it to life and create an atmosphere. Sketch the character(s) involved briefly, so readers get a picture. Set a timer. Stop after ten minutes and re read it – aloud is good (if you can). Make a few alterations. Then maybe read it to someone else. It's important to hear the sound of what you're saying. This helps the story to flow. It's also good practice to hear feedback, from a few people – not flattery, not uninformed or destructive. Constructive feedback. Hear it without being defensive. Take what's useful, ignore the rest.

Chapter 3   Plans are not lists

'Story is the journey you make, plot is the route you take.'[6]
'The best time for planning a book is when you're doing the dishes.'[7]

A beginning, middle and end – not necessarily in that order!

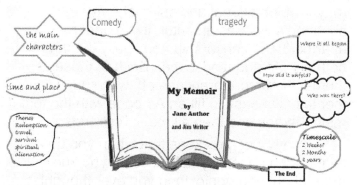

Sketch: Mindmapping – how to?

This is a Mindmap. A great tool for planning your book. See if you can answer some of the questions in the picture, in your own mindmap.

Doing a Mindmap[8] is a good way to begin planning your memoir. Tony Buzan created Mindmaps way back. I came across them in the 1970s.

---

[6] Paul Ashton, BBC Writer's Room
[7] **Agatha Christie**
[8] How to Mind Map: The Ultimate Thinking Tool. Tony Buzan (2002) Thorsons

You take an A4 sheet of paper, draw a small circle in the middle, then draw around four 'arms' going in four directions from that small circle. The aim is to collate, gather together, all the knowledge you have about a subject and get it onto one page. You can use it for any topic, but here we're going to use it for your memoir. There's probably about 4 main themes or subject areas in your memoir.

In mine, there was my own journey (physical, emotional and spiritual), my husband's work as an actor, living under apartheid and censorship and finally the land, both people and landscape. Each of those themes had more branches off, with sub themes. It's easy to fill an A4 page with the four main themes and then all the sub-strands.

Tony Buzan reckons that when you do a Mindmap on a topic you'll discover you know more about your topic, than you ever thought you did. In fact you could talk for twenty minutes to an hour on the topic by the time you've done your Mindmap.

I've just tried it on the subject of jigsaws. I know next to nothing about jigsaws, I've put together a few I suppose. But amazingly, I made a Mindmap which covered a whole page on the topic.

One branch was on types of jigsaw – children's (different age groups), adult jigsaws with complicated pictures of a thousand pieces; another branch was materials used to make them – wood, plastic, cardboard; another branch focused on pictures and graphics; another on the history of jigsaws. I could have gone on.

It's surprising what you know about a topic when you do a Mindmap about it. And you soon find out where you need to do some research too, to fill in the knowledge gaps.

When planning a memoir it doesn't need to start at point A and travel in linear fashion to point Z. Your story can start with a dramatic event and then can wander through a series of flashbacks or flash-forwards to tease out the story and keep the tension going, wetting the reader's interest, keep the reader turning the pages.

Unless you have a clear idea of the scope of your book - and starting with a story framework helps with that - you'll probably talk forever, about how you're going to write a book one day.

If you're serious about writing your story, think about where you want to start, where to finish (roughly). Write down five or six points/events that you want to cover between beginning and end.

Storyboarding

Another story planning technique – get a large piece of paper or card. Get some different coloured post-it notes. Write chapter headings and march the post-it notes across the card. Post-it notes are easy to pick up and move around. Now you can see how events flow in your story, move the notes around, have fun with it.

Back to the start ... where, when, what?

In Chapter 1 you were asked to come up with a starting point for your memoir. Have a notebook or an A4 pad and pen beside you.

Think of a date, or at least a year and a month in that year. What season was it? What was the weather?

WRITE IT DOWN

Now what country are you in - UK, Europe, Africa, Asia, America? The Mediterranean? Narrow it down some more – Wales? Zimbabwe? France? Brazil? Thailand? Greece?

WRITE IT DOWN

Now what town or city or village or rural area were you in when it all began?

WRITE IT DOWN

Narrow it down again? Were you on a train, on a bus or a Greyhound to New Mexico, in a car, in a plane? Starting a new life in a new country? Or were you in a room, in a house, a building or outdoors when the story began?

WRITE DOWN SPECIFICALLY
WHERE YOU WERE

So (for example), here you are in summer 2005, in rural England or backpacking across South Africa or starting a new vineyard in Italy or working in Johor Bahru, Malaysia. Maybe you were on a journey or tramping down a dusty road, in the red light district on the wrong side of town and something happened...

Describe what you can see. What's going on around you? What can you smell, hear? How do you feel – fear, elation, sadness?

Paint a picture so your reader feels like they are standing beside you, witnessing what you witnessed.

For example. You've decided to start with a particular event. First you launch into the story. You might have to give some back-story, about who you were at that moment in time. Who was with you?

Think in terms of 10- 20 chapters to start with (there'll probably be more, but you're just roughing it out for the present). Write a line or even a word or a person's name to show what that chapter will focus on.

Now you have an idea of the scope of your memoir. Next, think about where it will end – roughly. Give a date, a year, a month, a season, and a turning point that brings your whole story to a conclusion. Nothing's set, you can change it later. Just write it for now, to give yourself a time frame.

For my memoir, **A Hippopotamus at the Table**, the story started when I arrived in South Africa and ended when we left. Some stories are not going to be so simple, but it'll work better if you have a framework, within which your story will unfold. You can shorten or lengthen that framework later, when you see how it's all working out.

When writing my memoir, I didn't actually start at the beginning. The story began a few weeks after our arrival, while on a thousand mile car journey, from Johannesburg to Cape Town – because that was an interesting part of the story to grab readers' attention. Flashbacks were written as reflections about our arrival, our first encounters with apartheid, and to give some backstory.

Memoirs are often not linear at all, not chronological, they jump about. This is an art and although you must give readers credit for being able to follow your story wherever it goes, there's a risk of confusing the reader. If readers lose track, they put the book down and never finish it. So manage the links well.

I've started reading a few memoirs like that, by well-known or famous or very clever people. Then I've put the book down – I'll get back to it … but somehow I never do. So think about how the reader will follow the story, if you go down the non-linear route.

Exercise

Now it's your turn to draw a Mindmap. You can call it My Memoir (unless you have a working title in mind). Make a start and see what emerges. You're unlocking the doors to your memory and creativity as you draw. It will open the magic box to all that is involved in your story, your memoir. Far more than you realised. Remember my quote in Chapter 1?

'Most of us live in a chronic state of mental confusion, bewilderment, chaos and disorder...' [Sangharakshita]

What did Steven King say? About writing being like an archaeologist clearing away the debris, so the story can emerge. Mindmapping is a tool that can start the process of clearing the mud and sticks and stones from our minds. A framework can begin to emerge, on which to hang our story.

Here's a blank Mindmap for you to copy.

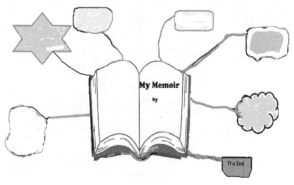

(like the one above)

Draw your own Mindmap on a large sheet of paper and start to fill it in. Put a circle in the middle and label it My Memoir. Create the main branches of your story and make each shape/title a different colour (if you've got some colouring pencils or felt-tips). Now make sub branches. Keep filling it in until you've put down everything you can think of, related to your story.

Now you have a plan, an idea of the scope of your project, a where-to-start, a where-to-finish and some of the main components and themes of your story. You've got your settings in hand too. You're ready to begin focusing in, on telling the story in more detail.

Chapter 4 Make your dialogue vibrant

> Of course I want to kill you," said Skulduggery.
> "I want to kill most people. But then where
> would I be? In a field of dead people with no
> one to talk to."
>
> **Derek Landy, Kingdom of the Wicked**

'*...who can remember the exact dialogue that took place at breakfast forty years ago? And if you can make up dialogue, change the name and hair colour of a character to protect the privacy of the living, or even as some memoirists do – reorder events to make the story work better, how is that different from fiction?*' Judith Barrington

Dialogue *in fiction* is created by the writer, between two (or more) fictional characters. They may speak in a way that imagined characters might speak, they may say things the imagined characters might need to say to move the story forward. Everything, both characters and dialogue is fiction, created in the mind of the writer. The writer will base this dialogue on other dialogues s/he has heard, on their own life experiences even, but the content, the events, the character of the speakers are invented.

Dialogue, *in memoir*, might *seem* to be made up, as the writer rarely has perfect recall of conversations from the past. However, the memoir writer has (usually) a reasonable recall of the persons speaking, their characters, appearance, circumstances, age, social status, their attitudes and their relationship to him or her, the writer, with whom they are in dialogue.

For example, in my book, when I wrote dialogue that was between myself and my then husband in 1975, I couldn't remember the exact wording. But I knew what we looked like, how we thought, what we knew and what our situation was at that time. I knew the way he spoke and the way the two of us interacted, the humour, the teasing, the way we were towards each other. Similarly with friends of different ages and acquaintances – I remember their characters, how they spoke, what their accent was and how they interacted with me and each other.

So when I write dialogue in any of my memoir writing, NO, it is NOT the same as fiction. I can stand behind what is being said and discussed and say, this is a close approximation of a conversation we would have had at that time. It's **not** the same as fiction-dialogue at all.

Think of a time [in the context of your memoir], when you had an important conversation with someone. This conversation highlighted your situation at the time or highlighted the way certain characters behaved, or gives the reader an insight into an event. It could be a heated exchange, a row between you and another, or someone demonstrated a vulnerability that you hadn't seen before.

Often what makes good writing is not what is said, what is in the foreground, it is the '*spaces in between*'. Pinter and Beckett were masters of this art. In *The Birthday Party* and *The Homecoming*, Pinter's characters show brilliantly our human struggle to communicate with few words spoken and many pauses in the dialogue. The silences are heavily laden, sometimes with hostility, sometimes grief or sadness, sometimes just boredom. Beckett too in *Waiting for Godot* uses silence to powerful effect. His dialogue is sparse and simple.

We think dialogue is about communicating. What's far more interesting is how dialogue is so often about NOT communicating. Body language in a scene will often convey much more. Remember, research shows that only 7% of our communication is verbal – the rest, the other 93%, is body language and facial expressions.

As a writer – how are you going to convey this? Are displays of anger gender-specific? When we're angry, sometimes our faces go red and frowning.

Some men may glower, clench their fists, punch a door, charge around, stamp out and down to the pub.

Women *tend* to be more passive, they're socialised to think displays of anger are 'unfeminine', to hide their anger – they will bang a door shout, cry, or just say something under-the-table bitchy. Or if they lose it completely, they may scream. This may be stereotypical but it's often (not always) how it works.

You may well have to play with the dialogue to convey a super-charged atmosphere, where someone is about to explode. Maybe everyone else in the room is nervous, but hiding it, because they can feel a storm coming, the build-up to something. Use body language and facial expressions as a way in to that.

Don't (as a rule) write too much dialogue, especially if it's not one of your strengths. In a writer's group years ago, I was told by someone who was further down the writing path than me,

'You've not enough dialogue, you need much more.'

I worked hard to put masses of dialogue into my chapters. Then I went to do a Professional Writing MA and my tutor said,

'Why have you got so much dialogue? Your strength is in your descriptive passages. Cut down on the dialogue!'

She was right and I went through my book slashing and burning, deleting masses of extraneous (dull) dialogue. I realised I must listen to *my own* thoughts, feelings, opinions about my writing, my own instinct - not always follow someone else's.

Writing good dialogue keeps words to a minimum and leaves so much unsaid. Just as in real life. If you listen to any conversation amongst a group of people, what creates atmosphere and highlights the existential pain is not how we communicate, it is how we don't.

Exercise (Part 1)

Writing good dialogue is a skill you can learn like any other. Some people can do it with ease, most of us have to work at it. Practise, practise, practise.

'... *nothing can break the mood of a piece of writing like bad dialogue'*. Anne Lamott[9]

So what should you do to improve your writing of dialogue?

Anne Lamott again:

'*You listen to how people really talk, and then learn, little by little to take someone's five minute speech and make it one sentence.'*

When people talk there's lots of umming and ahhing. Cut all that, it makes your dialogue too ... busy. The secret of good writing is always to keep paring down to the essentials.

While you're observing, look at body language. Have your characters get up and pace around the room, walk around the furniture, sit closer to one person, listening intently. Does their voice tone show contempt, a slight lip curl, a dismissive comment?

The Task. For the next few days, listen to how people talk to each other, really listen. What's their accent? Is there a regional dialect? Is English their first language? How will you write/convey that?

Do they talk in slang or in short sentences or in long rambling tracts? Do they talk over

---

[9] Bird by Bird. Some Instructions on Writing and Life. Anne Lamott (1995) Anchor Books

each other or leave sentences in the air, unfinished? Are they dominating or quiet and unassuming? Do you strain to hear what they say, as their voices are so soft, or are they loud and arm waving?

Exercise (Part 2)

When you get home, *set your timer for 15 minutes.* Write a page of some dialogue between you (as narrator) and some of the characters in your story. Where are you? What's the scene that's taking place? Think of it like writing a scene from a play. Make sure we know where in the room your characters are – sitting, standing, storming about, moving around objects in the room, picking things up, putting them down, looking out the window, patting the dog ... whatever. Place them in the space and in the reader's imagination.

Read it out loud, how does it sound? The usual mistake with dialogue is to make it too wordy. Cut it down. How do you convey emotion? With the facial expressions, a glance, a flush, a drawing down of the mouth? Imply or hint at the emotion - anger, love, sadness, frustration, boredom, contempt. For example.

He thumped the table, his eyes glaring. I jumped and pushed my chair back.

Or

The shock was too much for me, I turned from the window, tears in my eyes. James stepped round the chair and touched my shoulder awkwardly, then coughed and walked over to the bookshelf staring at the rows of books, his hands behind his back.

Reading it aloud shows up stilted dialogue. Each speaker's dialogue should be on a new line. Leave out descriptive adverbs such as '*she said crossly.*' Try showing different speakers with the character doing something.

For example

She glanced across the table.

'I'm not doing that, you can go to hell.'

He picked up the cigarette packet, took one and lit it.

'Why not?'

Another useful practice is to notice dialogue in the books you read. Stop when you reach some and notice how it is written, what does it do to the scene? Often there's a descriptive passage, then a short piece of dialogue, then more description. Dialogue breaks up long passages and brings you into the moment. It brings the scene to life. Notice the way that works.

Chapter 5 Your voice. The narrator.

'If you are a writer, give yourself permission to tell us who you are ...
.. the most interesting person in a memoir, we hope, will turn out to be the person who wrote it'[10]

How are you going to address your audience? Formal/non formal. Colloquial/non colloquial?

Voice is that most elusive of writer talents and it's essential to have it, if you want to bring your writing to life and catch the reader's attention. It's what reviewers and agents and publishers look for. An original voice. You. I can see you cringe into a corner – who am I? Who cares what I say?

Remember that famous quote, used by Nelson Mandela in his Presidential inauguration speech?

---

[10] William Zinsser, On Writing Well (1990) Harper Collins

'Your playing small does not serve the world. There is nothing enlightened about shrinking, so that other people won't feel insecure around you. We are all meant to shine as children do.'[11]

So find your voice and use it – you are not an observer of life, but a participant in it – or you wouldn't be wanting to write your memoir.

What is voice?

Think of your favourite writers – fiction or memoir – I'm thinking JR Tolkien, JK Rowling, Maya Angelou and that master of beautiful words in memoir Ryzard Kapucinsky. Then there's Bill Bryson; Nelson Mandela; Barack Obama; Dylan Thomas, Stevie Smith. These are some of my favourite memoir writers (got to the end of the book for a list of my 20 favourites). You'll have your own favourites.

Think of their writing style. What makes it unique? Is it intimate, casual, flippant, formal or colloquial? How do they come across to you the reader? How do they relay dialogue, description and character? All of that is a writing style, usually more or less original to that writer. That's voice.

How can you tell what's YOUR voice as a writer? That's harder. We can always talk about other people's strengths and weaknesses - it's much harder to point to our own.

---

[11] Nelson Mandela, quote from Marianne Williamson's *Our Deepest Fear.*

Here's **some key questions** to ask yourself, to help discover and strengthen your voice. If you are writing memoir the questions apply to *you personally*. If you're writing fiction they apply partly to you, partly to your main characters/ protagonists. Your reader must care about you or your main character(s), not necessarily *like* them, but be interested in their story.

1. What is the **dominant impression** of you being demonstrated? What is your main role in the story? What are your main goals and how do you go for them? What defines you in the writing? Organised; sloppy; angry; happy; depressed; moaning; cheerful; good-natured? Are you shy, quiet, bouncy, loud, confident or bombastic? Always an observer or the opposite? A natural leader or always in the background? When you were in school did you always have your hand up to answer the teacher's questions or did you hide out at the back of the class and keep your head down ... Or somewhere in between?

2. What is your **physical appearance**? Large? Stocky? Slim? Curvy? Messy? Fashionista? Well dressed? Hippy? Look-at-me-queen/ prince? Neat? Dread-locks? Crew cut? Long hair, short, trendy, bob? Beard? Moustache? Designer stubble? How would you describe yourself?

3. What is your **basic background**? Grew up where?

- Mansion or hovel? Palace or shack?

- Family life? Ordinary? Abusive? Wacky?
- Economic? Poor working class? Well-off?
- Education? Self-taught, higher degree?
- Status? High or low?
- Politics? Left, right, centre?
- Culture? African, Asian, White European?
- Music you liked - pop, classical, techno, heavy metal, soul, rock, punk, opera? Write a few notes.

4. Did you have **something dramatic happen** - as a child? Teenager? Young adult? Older adult? What effect did it have on you? Were you isolated and alone? Solitary or sociable? How will it affect your writing....?

5. **Hopes and dreams** - Will these be fulfilled? Was/is there something missing/lacking in your life?

6. What does your *actual* **voice sound like**? Loud, soft, confident, shy. What's your accent – regional; Mancunian; Welsh; Scottish; Belfast; RP (i.e. BBC British or Received Pronunciation)?

   Or, American Alabama; American Harvard; Australian; New Zealand; Nigerian; South African; Ghanaian; French; German; Spanish; Australian, Russian; Latvian...

   I could go on – each of these can be sub-divided into regional accents endlessly. I'm talking about how you speak English of course, how your nationality and spoken English will affect the way you write and the voice you write with.

Record your voice, reading a paragraph, on your mobile phone – play it back and listen, really listen. Get used to the sound of your voice. Try not to be over-critical. We often hate the sound of our own voices. We're not used to hearing them that's why.

If you briefly think these points through, you'll begin to see everything that shaped who you are today and how they affect how you write your story.

When I first started writing, I thought I had to eliminate my own voice, not write like I speak, be neutral. *No, no, no.* Let your own unique and wonderful voice be heard in your writing. That will catch the reader's attention, make them warm to you and want to see what happens to you.

In fiction it's important for the reader to empathise or identify with the lead character. In memoir, that's YOU. The reader must empathise with you in some way, be on your side.

EXERCISE – 10 minutes

Write a short paragraph. Set your timer, stop when it beeps. Put your pen down, Read it aloud.

Take an event from your teenage years. Write it as if you are in the mind of that teenager, how they look, think, feel. Teenagers (in my experience) are often very self-absorbed and think they know everything. Underneath all that bravado, they are still naïve and innocent. Was that how it was for you? Or did something happen that made you grow up too fast?

Pick an event that happened and describe it in the voice of the teenager you were. If it's something upsetting, go carefully, be kind to yourself. You can switch to something less emotionally charged if it's too difficult.

Finding your voice as a writer is about looking closely at who you are, your personality, appearance and background. How would you talk to friends? That's your voice. Of course we all talk to different people with a variety of voices. I remember knowing who my mother was talking to, when she answered the phone, by the voice she adopted.

Think about how you want to speak to your readers when you tell your story. The voice you start with should then be consistent from start to finish.

Chapter 6 Writing Humour

Humour in writing is a tricky thing to get right. One of my students (the one writing the revenge story) regularly had the whole group in fits of laughter. She was very surprised. She was not consciously writing humour, it just came naturally. We all looked forward to her readings during the course, as each time, we'd end up laughing. It was not obvious humour, not at all.

What was it about her writing that was so funny? She was writing about an office where she'd once worked, not an obviously comedic setting, although …. There was something about her descriptions of the characters – I remember one, where she described the objects on this guy's desk – she painted a picture of a guy obsessed with his own appearance and importance. It was hilarious. She did not mince words but neither were her descriptions nasty or unpleasant. It was the spare factuality of the description. The observational details she gave about the characters made them very funny.

Her quirky observations made us all laugh but not on purpose - she was stunned by the reaction of the group – she had no idea of her own comic writing talents.

How **you** do it will be different, how you'll write humour. It may be a natural gift, but if it isn't, you can learn it by following a few pointers. Like my group member, you might be surprised and find a talent you didn't realise you had.

'*I would say, as a rule of thumb, never aim to be funny. If you're not a comic, clown, comedian, or naturally funny person, who is always looking for and finding the humour in every situation, then it will sound forced and stilted.*

However, if a situation or experience you had at a time in the past, was amusing, then think objectively about the experience and pinpoint what it was you found funny. That will then be your focus as you recount the moment. Do not try to mold it into being funny, it will sound contrived. Just describe the moment and keep your focus on the core reason why you found it funny. Again carefully choose your vocabulary to aid and strengthen your core focus. Read it aloud to yourself. Does it make you smile? Yes? Then good, you've tapped into the humour of that moment.

Remember, if it makes you smile, then it will make other people smile. It might not make everyone smile but all humour is subjective.'
David Powell Davies. Actor/Writer/ Funny Man.

Here's some comedy writing techniques for you to watch out for in your analysis of why something is funny. You can practise noticing the categories of technique.

1. Observation/recognition/surprise

You lead the audience through a story, the kind of story they recognise from their own experience. Except you're leading them to a completely unexpected conclusion to the story. For example, talking about parking tickets, how much you hate them, slag off parking wardens, criticising councils. Then you go into a fantasy scenario where you obtain an AK47, black up and at 3 in the morning go round shooting out traffic cameras.

2. Opposites

Big and small, happy and sad. For instance, the 'class' sketch by the two Ronnies and John Cleese. They stand in line –

John Cleese , tall, haughty, in a bowler hat, black suit, rolled-up umbrella and upper class accent –

'I'm Upper Class. I look down on them.'
Ronnie Barker – medium height, stocky, casual dress. *'I'm Middle Class, I look up to him and down on him.'*
Ronnie Corbett – in a cloth cap and braces, – 'I'm Working Class.' He looks up at the other two –
'I get a pain in the neck.'
[Big laugh].

This sketch incorporates recognition, opposites. And lastly surprise – the rule of three. You expect him to say one thing and he says something completely different.

3. Incongruity/inversion

Turning things around, looking at them backwards, creates incongruity. Examples – a man in full clown costume sitting round the table with the cabinet at No 10 Downing Street. Teresa May dressed in a pink fru fru dress and red high heels walking in to McDonald's …makes you smile, yes?

4. Misdirection

Leading the audience 'up the garden path', You make it sound like the story's going one way, then at the last minute the direction changes completely.

5. Exaggeration

Fairly self-explanatory – going completely over the top to get a laugh. For instance, a male friend said this to me recently, rolling up his sleeves

'Look at those biceps – like chunks of wood, like Tarzan swinging in the jungle. You've never seen any that good.'

I laughed.

6. Misunderstanding

Most comedy sitcoms and situation comedies are riddled with this technique – a character says something, and is completely misunderstood. This is farce. Or someone overhears a conversation and draws the completely wrong conclusions. This leads the story one way, until everyone realises. Now all the threads of the story untangle and sort themselves out. A classic of course is Fawlty Towers (Basil Fawlty and Manuel)

7. Innuendos/Double Entendres

Saying one thing, but implying something else, often quite rude or smutty, Frankie Howard, Benny Hill or Kenneth Williams were all masters of this technique.

8. Bathos/pathos

The sublime to the ridiculous, it works by exaggerating the contrast between two things. For example, changing the setting for a scene, like making Macbeth into a sit-com, a comedy into gothic horror. Highlighting something incongruous in a sad scene or story. Charlie Chaplin was a master of this.

9. The rule of three

Lines 1 and 2 lead the audience to expect one thing. Line 3 is unexpected, a surprise. It can be (for example) a joke featuring an Englishman, an Irishman and a Scotsman, and the joke or surprise or punchline comes at number three, the Scotsman.

Or

- You tell a joke that sets up an expectation
- You reinforce that expectation.
- You break the expectation, change what happens.

'Most laughs come from surprise: the sudden unexpected event, the twist that you didn't see coming, the moment when the penny drops'.[12]

---

[12] Masterclass: Writing Comedy. Teach Yourself. Lesley Bown

10. Verbal comedy

Uses word play. There a many different forms and techniques. Here's a few of them:

- **puns** (a play on words to create a joke)
- **innuendo** it's a hidden hint (often sexual) that what your saying has one meaning on the surface and another one hidden beneath, A good example is the American early Hollywood actress, Mae West *'Is that a gun in your pocket or are you just pleased to see me.'* Double Entendres, are similar – something said has a double meaning.
- **Jokes, gags, running gags**, Jokes and gags are often one-liners designed to elicit a laugh. Or they can be a funny story, ending with a punch line. A running gag is when the joke or gag is repeated a number of times, throughout the story.
- **Malapropism** – created by either intentional or unintentional misuse of a word. The name comes from Mrs Malaprop in the play, The Rivals by Sheridan.
- **Clichés**. Clichés are well or over-used phrases or sayings in the English language. A listener expects a certain outcome for a cliché – the comedy writer changes the outcome unexpectedly - setting up a surprise.
- **Spoonerisms** – similar to malapropism but it is more sounds than words. The sounds have been incorrectly (and unintentionally) changed.
- **Mixed metaphors**

Well-known clichés are mixed up, apparently unintentionally, for example:
'like a frog caught in the headlights', (instead

of a rabbit).

11. Visual comedy,

Mime falls into this category – Charlie Chaplin and Laurel and Hardy were masters. Chaplin had his hat, his cane, baggy trousers and a funny walk. Laurel and Hardy, tripped up, fell over things, walked into doors, dropped things, sat on absent chairs – the list is endless. Why do we laugh – because we've done many of these things ourselves? Visual comedy leads into -

12. Physical comedy (eg. Mr Bean)

The protagonist has accidents, is assaulted, chairs collapse, things don't work. We laugh at the incongruous falls and slips that people have on those Candid Camera videos.

* * *

This is just a brief glance into the world of comedy writing. There's plenty of books on Google or Amazon – look at some of the titles on various sites.

EXERCISE – 10 minutes

Think of a scene from your story so incongruous, so amusing, it always makes you laugh, or at the very least smile.
Chances are it'll do the same for your reader.
Remember comedy is often light relief, after tragedy or something sad happening. It breaks the tension. Not only does comedy lift the atmosphere, but also, through contrast, it highlights the sad scene/ the tragic part.
Sometimes laughing and crying are closely bound together and comedy makes tragedy easier to cope with.

Set your timer, stop when it beeps. Put your pen down, Read it aloud.

- Did it make you smile?
- What about it was funny?
- Was it the setting, the place?
- Was it the people, what someone said?
- Was it a misunderstanding?
- Was it a verbal mistake? An accent? A wrong word used?

  - Was it the clothes someone wore? Incongruous? A funny hat? Big ears?

  - Was it a look? A trip up?

  - Was it a joke? A cultural misunderstanding?

  - Or something else – try and explain what made you laugh?

Do a short analysis. This is to help you identify some key points about how to use humour in your writing. Then re-write it, big it up, exaggerate, to make it even funnier. Watch comedians, like Dawn French, Victoria Wood, Tommy Cooper, Tracey Ullman, Michael McIntyre tell stories – how they describe a scene like going to the dentist or the shops and everyone is roaring with laughter all the way through.

Chapter 7 How to describe people

> Description begins in the writer's imagination but should finish in the readers.
>
> **Stephen King: On Writing**
>
> Just don't pretend you know more about your characters than they do, because you don't. Stay open to them. It's teatime and all the dolls are at the table. Listen. It's that simple.
>
> **Anne Lamott: Bird by Bird**

Read Stephen King's book, *On Writing*[13]. The book is part memoir, part observations on the writing process. He has some strong opinions about character description. He does not believe you should describe people's clothes or appearance too much. Rather you should leave it to the imagination of the reader, a few broad brushstrokes - not every spot and pimple. He gives examples and I can see his point clearly.

He creates a scene - a dark bar, throws in a few people - you don't want the story held up by long descriptions of those characters - they are there to paint a picture, create the atmosphere, perhaps they'll be part of the plot, perhaps not, we don't know yet.

---

[13] On Writing: A Memoir of the Craft. Stephen King (2012) Hodder

The thing is, Stephen King describes his own writing processes (which is useful to hear about), but we all have different ways to create on that blank page in front of us. After reading this fascinating book, I think Mr King would probably agree with me. He's not writing a rulebook for writers, rather he's musing about his own writing processes and trying to see how it all works. And I thank him for that.

But he's talking about incidental fictional characters that might populate a scene, give it colour and shape. We're writing about people we know or knew. One of whom is of course ourselves. *'Whatever the genre, strong, memorable main protagonists are important'*. That's you. Don't turn yourself into a piece of the background. We the readers want to know why you did what you did, how it felt and what you looked like.

The characters we present and interact with should do the same. They need (I think) more than a brief one-liner. Maybe not all at once, maybe drip-fed into the story here and there. But these are real people and for me, I like to picture them early on. Maybe it's a woman thing, but I also like to know what they're wearing, what kind of style they had. Were they fat, thin, tall, short, spotty, old, young and so on?

I'll describe my father as an example:

He was 5 foot 11" well built, thick, dark-brown hair, large brown eyes. My aunt Beryl talked about him, a couple of years ago, when she was 90. She'd been my mother's college pal and was with her, when she met my Dad, soon after the end of the Second World War. They were all in their early twenties.

'He was so good looking,' she shook her head. *'I wouldn't have liked to take him on. When he walked into a room, all the women there turned their heads.'*

She compared his looks to James Stewart or Gregory Peck, Hollywood male stars of his era. I guess he knew it too, His hands were always beautifully manicured and his clothes were immaculate – dark blue blazers, grey slacks. He was immensely charming too.

My mother must have been the envy of other women - not that she ever gave that impression - she was a looker too, blue eyes and long blonde hair in the style of Veronica Lake, when she met him.

My father flew flying boats and bombers for the RAF in WWII at the age of 18 and 19. At 20 he'd taken part in the bombing of Dresden and had lost quite a few of his friends.

What effect did all this have on his personality later? It must have been a dark one. Outside the home he was popular, successful. Inside, he operated from a Victorian rulebook and was sometimes subject to dark rages. I loved and feared him in equal measure.

That's a whole paragraph of description about my father. Do you now have a clear picture of who he was and what he looked like? And a feeling for his personality too?

Exercise

Take a moment – a ten-minute exercise – set your timer.

Describe someone you knew well from childhood. What did they look like, how did they dress? Pick something they wore that really illustrates their sartorial style. For example, old scuffed brown leather shoes, six-inch red stilettos or new white Nike trainers.

Pick a facial feature – the nose is a good one – broad and flat, small and thin, large and hooked?

Facial expressions - do they smile easily or frown a lot? Do their eyes dart around, nervously, is their smile reflected in their eyes? Do they carry a mood around with them – jolly, cheerful, dark, sad?

Now if you can, take another ten minutes. Think of another character. Describe them physically and a key aspect of their personality, a quick sketch. You'll be using a modified version of these descriptions in your memoir.

* * *

Here's an extract from one of my favourite memoirists Ryzard Kapuscinski:[14]

Ghana 1958   First he describes the place. Then

'And finally; the most important discovery – the people. The locals. How they fit the landscape, this light, these smells. How they are as one with them. How man and environment are bound in an indissoluble, complementary, and harmonious whole.'

---

[14] The Shadow of the Sun. My African Life. Ryszard Kapuscinski (2001) Penguin Press

Chapter 8 Time and Place

TIME

What country? Who is in government? What precise weeks or months, are covered in your story?

Which world events? You know what country you were in when the events in your memoir took place, don't you? You know what town you were in, you know what road you were on and you know where the house was? [Except if you were a kidnap victim of course].

Write yourself and your characters into the time and place, even if the world events are a distant backdrop.

Do you know who was president, or prime minister of the country you were in and what was happening in the world? Imagine writing a memoir that starts in Nov 2016 without referring to **Brexit** or **Donald Trump**? Or writing your story starting in 1966, without mentioning **The Beatles**, or in America 1972, without mentioning

Richard Nixon and **Watergate**, or UK set in 1990, without mentioning *Margaret Thatcher* and *the Poll Tax riots*. Anyone who was an adult at the time, knows what they were doing on September 11, 2001(*9/11*), when *The World Trade Centre* in New York was attacked – you wouldn't leave that out would you? Or if your story was set in *Syria 2015* and you didn't mention Assad and the civil war; or Egypt set in 2011, without mentioning **The Arab Spring**, or the year and month when **Princess Diana** was killed (August *1997*)? Even if at the time you did not feel the events were important or relevant to you, mentioning them can give context to your story.

It doesn't have to be only big events either. A memoir writer in one of my groups went away and researched the year certain events happened to her – political events of which she had no understanding at the time – she was a child and her father a politician. She included some of this research into her early chapter and suddenly it all came to life, it became fascinating, it gave context to what had happened to her.

My memoir was set in South Africa 1975-77, a time of full apartheid and censorship. It would be unthinkable not to talk about those circumstances and conditions in my story.

PLACE

You know all about the place where your memoir is set don't you? Or do you? Do you remember the details? Do you need to do some research?

I went back to South Africa, for the first time in 30 years, in 2007 to jog my memory for my book. Of course so much had changed. Apartheid was gone, Nelson Mandela was free, which was brilliant and I returned to see the beautiful country where I'd once lived. I wanted to get a sense of place, to look at the landscape, travel around the amazing, rugged valleys and mountains, gaze again at Table Mountain and the Atlantic Ocean, so my descriptions would be alive and vibrant. I took a backpacker minibus along the Garden Route, on the east side of South Africa, from Cape Town to Hermanus to the Tsitsikamma Forest along the Indian Ocean side. The bus drove across the amazing lagoon in Knysna and on up to Port Elizabeth and Grahamstown and then Durban. This was a route we had travelled in our little VW beetle in 1976.

I had held all these places in my memory but wanted to press 'refresh' on my brain's computer.

Of course when I look back now, to that time of research, I had changed just as South Africa had changed. That journey was a new story, a new adventure in itself.

To describe the dramatic landscape of the Karoo – a vast stretch of semi-desert we had to cross to get from Jo'burg to Cape Town, I used dialogue to give a sense of place:

'The car chugged on through the endless flat landscape. …

'How far to go now?'

I had the map spread out on my lap.

'It's nearly five hundred miles more of Karoo and then we go over the mountains. Then it's another four hundred to Cape Town.'

EXERCISE

Describe a ***place*** that is integral and important to your story – a town, a house, a room. Pick out some interesting details. Stand there (shut your eyes, use your imagination) and look around. What can you see? Who else is there – what do they look like? What is their relationship to you? How are you dressed? What are the colours, smells around you? Imagine you are a Set Designer and Props Mistress/Master. If you're in a room, what size is it? How is it laid out? What furniture tables, chairs, book cases, boxes on the floor, pictures on the walls, windows ....? What's on the table – bowls of soup, paperwork – scattered, messy or neat?

Now set your clock. Take 10 minutes. Write half a page using the set you designed above. Get your characters to move around the furniture, look out the window, pick up a book on the table, take out their cigarettes and put the packet on the table, stare at one of the pictures on the wall – all while in a dialogue with someone else in the room.

When your alarm starts peeping STOP. Now read what you've written out loud. This is a reminder that when you write dialogue, people are not floating around in a void.

When you have gathered your information, then you can see the importance of time and place. Think about your story – hone in on where it begins. Finding information is so easy today – you just Google it or Bing it or whatever search engine you use.

Make a bullet-point list of the events around that time, in the place where you were. Look at several sources, bearing in mind that some sources reflect conservative or left wing opinions or contain propaganda. How does it fit with what you recall? Check with people you know who remember the events described.

For this exercise take an hour. Fact gathering takes time. This is a start.

Here's what can happen if you don't double check your memory of background events that are integral to your story.

I did not check the exact date of a particular world news event, when I was writing my story – I just ploughed on. Then when I was reviewing the 'finished' manuscript I finally got round to looking it up. I'd threaded together about 5 or 6 chapters into a smooth cohesive narrative, with this event in the middle. It was then I discovered the exact *date* of this event I'd referred to. I was a month out and to change it would completely mess up the entire thread I'd put together. My memory was at fault.

In the end, I had to rejig about 10

chapters, rewriting all the links and moving chapters around to make the story work. It took months. This wasn't the only factual data problem I encountered - an important source for the continuity of my story did not turn up until 5 months before publication date – dragged out of my ex, who '*hates looking at the past.*' Again I had to re-write large sections of the story to link the events and story together.

To sum up, think carefully about what happened – check all your dates as you go along.

- Do your best to obtain verification of dates, not just of world events but also of local events, life events – check with family members and friends (where relevant).

- Find your tickets, check newspapers, check old diaries.

- Check with people you may still be in touch with. You can do some of it as you go along, but make it part of your advanced planning if you can. In the end the best laid plans …

Chapter 9 Emotional rescue

'.. I'll come to your emotional rescue,' as the Rolling Stones' song goes. Sometimes our writing requires *emotional rescue*. We tell a story but fail to include the full spectrum of emotions that can bring life into our writing. There's the basic list: love/hate; sad/happy; anger/calm; bored/excited; tired/energetic; powerful/ powerless and all the variations on these, the subtle undertones.

If you're writing a scene, *show* emotions when you describe an interaction - between the character and you or someone else. A direct confrontation is easy to 'show' as it's 'out there', visible. You can watch it unfold, slamming doors, shouting, raised voices, smashing things, fists clenching and glaring eyes. But not all confrontations are out in the open. Some are under the surface, quite hidden, some are slow burning. How are you going to highlight/reveal them? The carefully blank faces, the tight smiles, the quick flash of a glance, the heavy silences,

Sometimes the unfolding story can build

emotion gradually, layer upon layer, without having to be revealed directly. Or sometimes a few broad, brush strokes are enough to point up the tension between two characters. If you're writing memoir, you'll have intimate knowledge of the different emotions going on at various points of the story. Just remember to bring your own feelings and emotions in to play - not just those you observe in others in order to bring your scenes to life. The same applies to writing fiction, but in that case you are using imagination.

When I started writing my first memoir (many years ago) I thought I'd write the story as an observer and keep myself in the background. Feedback in writer's groups was often '.... *but we can't see you, we don't know what you're feeling*.' You can't just be an observer - it doesn't work, the writing doesn't come to life. You have to put yourself in there. It means you have to be vulnerable, that's what I was avoiding in the early days of my writing.

The best memoirs lift the reader into the time and place, seeing the sights and colours, smelling the smells. It's important also that the reader identifies with the narrator through revelations about feelings. You can't if you portray yourself as a cardboard cut-out.

Shut your eyes and immerse yourself in the scene you're describing - what are you feeling now and now and now? Before you start writing, you might think you can't remember. Sometimes it might take you days, weeks or months, to psyche yourself up to write a particular scene.

Then, when the stew has finished cooking, one day you'll sit down and start writing and a miracle happens. You'll close your eyes and see it all unfolding. You'll be able to picture the room or scene, smell the smells, breathe the air and feel the emotions involved. The trick is to reveal your own emotions *and* those of the other characters present – but first you have to find these emotions, in yourself.

EXERCISE

Choose a scene with under the surface emotional content – it should be emotionally charged. Focus on YOUR feelings. Now go deeper – remember there's an iceberg underneath – most of us, most of the time are aware only at a surface level of the emotions that are driving us. So don't just think –'*I was upset,'* go below that. Maybe you were angry, hurt, raging, irritated, sad, grief-stricken or joyful – give the emotion a strong clear word. Then demonstrate it, don't explain.

Now write out the paragraph and make sure, we the readers, can see and hear that emotion. Don't overstate it, being quite subtle often works. What was the trigger for the emotion – who else was in the room? Was it something they did or didn't do? Said or didn't say? To you or to someone else? Or maybe it's someone else's emotion you want to describe. How were they handling it? What was the effect on you?

Here's something I wrote, an example. A story from childhood.

*I was just tucking my dolly in her carrycot.
Her hair was parted in the middle and pulled
back into bunches with tight elastic bands, her
fringe clipped in a straight line – just like mine.
Mum and Dad and all of them were in the other
room – I could see them down the corridor,
talking and laughing. My dolly's carrycot rested
in a thin blue metal frame on the floor. I can still
see it. Michael came running in. He rushed at
my dolly in her carrycot, knocked her flying. He
stopped and looked at me with those big blue
eyes, his mouth pink and cupid.*

*Rage filled my heart, beating loudly in my
chest. My small fists clenched at the side of my
blue smock dress. I shook my head. Michael
was just walking off, leaving my dolly sprawled
on the floor, going back towards the doorway,
uncaring, already forgotten.*

*I bent down and picked up the cot frame
and charged, hitting him on the head with it and
he fell forwards. He lifted his head and his
mouth was wide as wide, a big roar came out of
his mouth. So loud. Mummy appeared.*

'What happened?'

'Michael fell over…'

*He was still roaring, as he sat up and his
chubby finger was pointing at me, his voice
quavered through the sobs…*

'She hit me, she hit me.'

*'No I didn't. He fell an' banged his head.
Knocked my dolly over.' I grabbed my dolly
from the floor and fussed over putting her back
in the carrycot.*

'Anna hit me Mummy. Whaaaaa….'

'No I didn't. You fell over.'

She grabbed us both by the arms and marched us out into the other room.

'He's got a cut, it's bleeding'. Someone pointed at Michael's forehead. They all turned to look at me, the guilty party.

I looked at them all defiantly. 'I didn't hit him.' I thrust my chin forward, daring them, defiant.

My mother looked at me, her eyes narrow. I avoided her eye and looked at the floor.

'What did you hit him with?'
'I didn't hit him, I didn't '

Lots of possibilities for writing that scene and highlighting the intense emotions without explaining. Not once do I say 'she felt' or' he felt'. What emotions were displayed without being stated – anger, rage, hurt, shock, defiance, guilt, shame, irritation, exasperation?

Now it's your turn.

Think of ONE scene from your story, where there were strong emotions at play. Are they out in the open or hidden? Write a short paragraph. Take up to 10 minutes. Set your timer, stop when it beeps. Put your pen down and read it aloud.

Chapter 10 Using the senses

Bringing a scene to life involves using the senses. Colour sound smell - don't forget to include it all.

The smell of summer rain on grass after a warm day, seeing the colours of the new leaves in my garden (red maple, crab apple blossom, pale greens) as spring moves forward, hearing the soft breeze rustling the leaves of the trees in a wood, the slightly metallic smell of exhaust fumes on a busy London street, seeing the pollution haze over the city, hearing the sound of a lorry rattling past, the smell of onions frying, coffee brewing, cigar smoke, hearing a helicopter circling overhead, seeing a red umbrella on a grey cold wet London day, a lake reflecting the willows on its banks, seeing the colours in a Cape Town sunset across the Atlantic, seeing women in bright red saris at a bus stop in India.

The senses bring a scene to life, bring the reader there - I bet when I mentioned frying onions you could smell them. That's all you have to do, mention them. No long flowery detail and it's like freshening up a room with a new pot of paint.

I nearly forgot another of the senses – taste. Why are cooking programmes so popular? We watch them and salivate with the celebrity chefs - imagine eating a slice of those beautiful cakes, like works of art - light sponges or pastries that would melt in your mouth....

So next time you're reading a book or writing a scene - look out for SMELLS, SIGHTS, SOUNDS AND TASTES. If you're the writer put them in - just a sketch, a light touch and see how it transforms the scene.

If you're the reader, look out for them and how lightly or detailed is the description. What's the effect on you the reader? Try it - describe a flower, the taste of candyfloss, the smell of the sea. Avoid clichés.

EXERCISE

Take a scene from somewhere in your memoir, something that happened – in a kitchen, on a beach, in a street somewhere. Who's there with you – is it hot or cold? Is the air fresh and clean or dusty and humid? What can you smell – ozone or jasmine or sweat, delicious food cooking or open sewers; wet dog; dust; rain; a smell of pigs; petrol; curry; ozone; a cake baking; old books? Here's a quick story I wrote, using the timer, to illustrate what I've been talking about. I was in India. It was breakfast time and I was craving an egg. . . .

Example - Breakfast in India.

I looked up and down the dusty street - it was hotting up. The cool early morning mist had lifted and the sun was beginning to burn. I was wearing a pale blue cotton shirt over knee-length, tan, cotton trousers, because as the day wore on, I couldn't bear anything but loose cotton next to my skin. My green army camouflage hat shaded my face and dark sunglasses kept the glare away from my eyes.

Crate-laden, horse-drawn carts vied on the narrow road, with beat-up cars, vans, a few SUVs and bright yellow tuk-tuks beep beeping their horns. Their tourist passengers hung on grimly, while they swerved through the traffic. I knew how it felt - like one more swerve and you'd tumble out from the wide-open sides. Horns honked and blasted, men shouted, crates rattled. India is rarely quiet and in the towns and cities, it's a mad cacophony of constant noise.

I went to cross the road and jumped back to avoid the large, milky-brown cow with long curved horns that emerged from behind a van. Sacred cows wander around busy streets untouched. Whether you're a pedestrian or vehicle, they're another hazard to watch out for.

I could see the street stall on the corner across the road, the portly man standing behind his griddle. He sold fried eggs and chapatti. He was fat, dark brown and frowning, wearing a grubby white vest, that he wiped his hands on here and there. I could see him breaking an egg onto the hot round griddle in front of him and pouring some floury white mix like a pancake *next to it. He spread the mix as thin as paper on the griddle and then expertly he flipped it over to brown the other side. Then the egg – breaking the yoke and swirling it with his spatula and flipping that over too. A thin man, wearing a blue and white dhoti and bright green shirt, was waiting patiently. I approached – I love Indian food, but the thought of another bland dhal curry and rice for breakfast …. I stepped carefully over a big round splat of cow dung on the roadside – you didn't want to tread on one of those in sandals or you'd be feeling the rich brown dung squirting in between your toes – and the aroma – phew!*

I nodded to him and he nodded back. He knew what I wanted – I wanted that sizzling fried egg wrapped in a roti with the grease running down my bare arm as I bit into it – all for the equivalent of around 25 pence. I could smell the hot, floury chapatti and fried egg, as he handed it to the man in front of me, who was holding out a few rupees. I smiled, as he broke my egg and dumped a spoonful of the floury mix beside it onto the hot plate. His face was impassive as he spread it with his spatula. My turn I thought, my eyes fixed on the griddle.

Actually that took me about 25 mins to write, including revising and editing. Before I began, I was not aware that this event was in my memory. Suddenly, I could see myself on that street quite clearly, smell the smells and hear the sounds. If you find you get carried away too and write for more than your ten minutes – that's fine. If the muse is upon you, let it run for a bit. That's the fun of writing. I hope the story illustrates how to write sounds, smells and colours and the effect on you the reader, in bringing the story to life.

Now it's your turn - set your timer for 10 minutes – when it starts beeping then put your pen down (unless you're on a roll). Read it aloud.

Remember – **SMELLS, SOUNDS, SIGHTS, TASTES** – that's what you want to focus on with this exercise.

Chapter 11 Facing your dragons

Writing Trauma and Abuse

Many of us have experienced trauma and abuse either as children or adults. Maybe in the telling of your story, you will need to refer back to such a time. Maybe it is a part of the time frame you have chosen to write about. Telling about trauma is revisiting a time of great pain and can feel like you are witnessing or experiencing the trauma or abuse again.

I was discussing my father's occasional violent rages with a family member one day. She too had experienced it as a teenager. *'But'* she said, looking at me as she was departing, *'I'm **not** a victim.'*

This statement comes from a fear of 'victim-blaming', a well-known phenomenon, where instead of blaming the perpetrator for acts of abuse, society often blames the victim – somehow he/she did something to deserve the violence, and therefore 'brought it on themselves' by their undefined actions, by their 'weak' or 'different' or 'criticised' personalities'. Or by remembering it or referring back to the abuse, instead of 'moving on', you are somehow at fault. People say 'Forget about it'. 'Put it behind you.' 'Let it go!'

Victims of abuse are often either disbelieved or encouraged to stop talking about it. If we can minimise what happened, sweep it under the carpet, hide it from view, then everyone can pretend such nasty things don't happen in their world.

The perpetrator might be a significant family member, a well-known person, an important member of the community. It's as if, the most important thing is, that the victim will damage that person's standing or reputation by 'dwelling' on it or talking about the abuse or going public.

The fact that you, the victim, have been damaged by that person's actions is sometimes dismissed as of less importance than maintaining the status quo, not making a scene. In some cases, the perpetrator will be left free to carry on abusing further victims. Don't make a fuss. Keep quiet. Don't, whatever you do, let anyone think you are a 'victim'.

In other words, what you, as 'a victim,' have suffered is dismissed. You are of lesser importance than the good of the group, whether it's family, social group, community, school. If by speaking up or speaking out, you are damaging one or more of those groups, you need to keep quiet, keep your voice low and keep it all hidden.

If you, as memoir writer, are going to talk about, reveal or discuss things that happened to you in the past – whether it's an unavoidable trauma, like a car accident or illness or whether it's abuse caused by a person or persons, to you as a child or adult, first remember it's not your fault. Either there's been an accident or the person who is responsible is/was the abuser. You *were* a victim of whatever/whoever it was. Second being a victim is not a crime, it's not a sign of weakness or failure.

In Japan when a ceramic is broken it is repaired with a special lacquer mix of gold, silver or platinum. The process is called *kintsugi*. The object may be covered in cracks but they're all now gold filigree – which adds to the beauty of the object. 'The philosophy behind the technique is *to recognise the history of the object and to visibly incorporate the repair into the new piece instead of disguising it.'*[15] *(My italics!)*

If you were a victim, you are also a survivor. The rich tapestry of the stories you have to tell, make you the interesting person you <u>are. Survivors are stronger</u> and more beautiful

[15] Kintsugi: the Art of Broken Pieces

because they have survived.

Someone spoke to me once about the victims of domestic abuse that I was working with. '*They must like it, or why would they put up with it?*' This was a shocking thing to say, born of ignorance and a dismissal of a victim's worth. It took a little while, but I taught that person to realise the wrong thinking behind that statement - the reasons survivors stay, the way they have been coerced, made to feel worthless both verbally and physically, the way their friends and family have been driven away, so they no longer have anyone to turn to for help.

Perpetrators of abuse are groomers and manipulators, who often target not just the vulnerable but also those who have qualities that society values, like empathy and compassion. They use the targeted 'soon-to-be victims' own good qualities against them, to weave a web of undermining and control. In reality anyone can become a victim to the controlling behaviour of the abuser. It's not just the vulnerable who are targeted by abusers.

As adults, it would seem we are responsible for our own actions. Obviously children (in particular) are not responsible for violence perpetrated against them physically or mentally (and by children I mean anyone under 18). Violence is *always* the adult's responsibility, not the child's.

But people can be vulnerable in many ways, whether they are old or young. They might be mentally vulnerable for many reasons - disabled or pregnant or caring for small children or animals. *Anyone* using violence or threat of violence or manipulation to control another is abusive and entirely responsible for their own actions.

Looking at the dictionary definition of a 'victim' –

Dictionary definitions of 'victim'.
Apart from the usual definitions about victims of crime ie. a person harmed, injured, or killed as a result of crime, accident, or other event or action, I found these:
A person who has come to feel helpless and passive in the face of misfortune and ill-treatment. [Google Dictionary].
A person who has suffered a tragedy. A person who is wounded. A person who has been tricked. Someone who has been hurt or damaged. Someone who has had something bad happen to them.

My definition - a victim is someone who is or was vulnerable (due to circumstances) and unable to defend themselves. They have been subjected to different kinds of violence, threat of violence or extreme manipulation, by a person who wants to force or coerce them to do *their* will or behave in a certain way or punish them for imagined 'wrong-doing'.

What my family member was afraid of, was the perception of a victim as someone who is 'weak' - therefore being seen as not able to be a strong, capable fully functioning and successful person. In her mind, in order to come across as strong, no long term effects, insecurities, anxieties or mental health issues must ever be revealed - nothing that could make you appear to be a victim under that definition. You must never be seen to be anything other than competent and efficient and fully functional in the game of life. Maybe a large majority of people think like that.

And then there's the real world ….

It might take a long time for you to write about *your* trauma and/or abuse. Fiction writers can use a third party character to describe their experience of abuse. Memoir writers have to face it head on, or leave it out and pretend it never happened. But (in my view) this may diminish the depth of your story. You'll always know that you've written your story with something missing. It might take months or years until you're ready to write about it. Some turn to alcohol or drugs to damp down the feelings.

I took me 30 years to write about the loss of my baby, late in pregnancy - to sit down and start writing about how it happened.

Be careful to whom you choose to show your first writings about what happened. I showed the chapter to someone who I thought would be fairly 'neutral', a fellow writer. I was afraid it might come across as mawkish and miserable. Unfortunately, I chose someone who had no real idea how to respond. Her kindly meant feedback felt patronising and dismissive. The person didn't mention the quality of the writing. What I had wanted was commentary on the writing, *not* sympathy for the traumatic event (perhaps I expected too much). When you choose someone, give them a clear idea of what you want. Remember that your trauma has an effect on them. They will have reactive feelings which they will often try to manage by being 'nice' to you.

Writing about trauma *can be* therapeutic (so I'm told). But my view is that therapy may be a by-product. If you're serious about writing, you're not doing it for 'therapy',

Think about why you want to write your story – do you want to get published? In other words are you wanting to be taken seriously as a writer? Are you writing to 'entertain,' enlighten or to let others know that they are not alone? Is it because you hope that revealing your experience of trauma can help others who have experienced similar things? Can you tell the story openly, without being over dramatic or over sentimental? Are you ready for that?

If you want a scene to come to life, you have to bite the bullet, because what you want is to increase reader identification with the main character (i.e. YOU). Reader identification sells books. Writing the story simply is often enough, you don't have to embellish, exaggerate or over-dramatise it. The facts speak for themselves. It's never more important to follow the maxim 'show don't tell', than when writing about trauma and abuse. Or maybe 'show and tell' is a better way to put it. Some information may be needed to set the scene, but don't use it to shy away from being there in the writing.

It's said so often it's almost a cliché - '*writing trauma is therapeutic*'. My answer is *Hmmmm... maybe, maybe not...?* I've always found trauma difficult and painful to write about, like some kind of self-torture, re-traumatising yourself by reliving the event. What about afterwards, when it's done? For me it's a bit like going to the dentist for a filling. Once it's done, I come out feeling relief that it's over…. Is that therapy?

Bringing trauma and abuse 'out into the light of day' by writing it down *can* help to resolve or let go of some of the issues. It depends. Usually, years of real therapy are needed to do that. You don't always want to dwell on the traumatised past. You want to turn your back on it. Look to the future.

However, sometimes in order to heal the past, you MUST revisit it, examine it from different angles, realise you were a victim, but you survived. Then you might be able to move forward and let go - when you've come to a certain place where that's possible. That place is different for everyone, your 'moving on' point is unique to you. Accept that. Respect your own self-knowledge.

Some rules for writing about trauma or abuse.

1. Tell the story simply without being mawkish or over-sentimental. Don't go into over-dramatic detail. Keep the writing spare and factual, although you can highlight the effect on your inner life. Show what happened without too much comment. . This will make your account all the more powerful.

2. Take care of yourself – only write about it when you're ready (it can take many years, to be ready). Stop when it becomes overwhelming. You can push yourself sometimes if you need to (only you know). Remember writing about the trauma or abuse can often feel like being 're-victimised'.

3. Be careful who you share or discuss or show the writing to, *the first time*. Choose carefully. You may not get the reaction you hope for. After that it gets a bit easier.

4. Get dispassionate feedback from other readers and writers about what you've written about. You are opening up and

making yourself feel vulnerable. But remember you survived. Talking about it means you're ready to move on or at least forward.

5. Think about the target audience, the readers of your memoir. Will they be moved, sad, angry when they read of your experiences? Face it, often readers buy books to experience all that. They like the real life drama. Let the story unfold naturally.

6. ***Remember - inspire yourself to face your dragons!***

Exercise
Set the alarm for 10 minutes. Write without stopping.

Take a short scene from the trauma/abuse that you have been a part of and write it for readers as if they are standing next to you, so they see unfolding what you see. If that's too hard, imagine you are reading it to a trained counsellor or a close friend.

Give yourself love and respect. Stop if you need to. Read it back to someone you trust or just aloud to yourself.

Chapter 12 Story Telling

Whether a story makes you laugh or cry, a good story immerses you in a different world and takes you away from the cares of your present.

'After nourishment, shelter and companionship, stories are the thing we need most in the world.' **Philip Pullman**

Ten points to remember in the art of story-telling and writing narrative.

1. A good plot and well-defined characters, brought to life by dialogue. Structuring a narrative is the most important thing you'll do. There's the narrative thread, unfolding story, for the whole book. Then chapter by chapter, building to climactic moments, creating dialogue and developing characters.

Emotional content Think about the emotional impact of what happened to you. You really want the reader to 'get' that, to be involved from the start. The emotional content for all the other characters involved comes next, how it develops and how they interact with you and each other.

2.   **Starting point.** Begin at a really interesting point in your story – a pivotal moment. The story should grip the reader from the opening sentence. Then work back, showing how the story got to that point.

3.   **Empathy with the narrator/protagonist** – in memoir, that's you. This is vital to keep up reader interest in carrying on reading so they really want to know what happens to you.

4.   **Mood changes** – that's not *your* mood, it's the mood changes of the story. If you have something dramatic happen, which carries on for a few chapters until it's resolved, maybe you need a chapter where everyone calms down, here and there.

5.   **How to end a chapter?**   Each chapter should end in such a way that the reader HAS to turn to the next page to find out what happened next. The links between chapters should flow smoothly.

When I wrote my first memoir, my editor told me. 'It's like a series of anecdotes'. So I went back and re-wrote beginnings and endings of chapters so the story flowed more smoothly.

6.   **Your story is unique**, whatever the

genre. Build the reader's involvement slowly, take them down a few tangents. Don't reveal it all straightway, so it's not clear where the story's going. Keep some surprises for the end. Build the reader's anticipation.

7. **Setting** is important, culture, country, rural, urban. Your story will start/end in a specific place. Think about the place and how the characters move around the objects – it's like writing a scene for a play.

8. **Colour, sound smell**. Make your references to these unusual and un-clichéd. Don't for example refer to the *sparkling turquoise* sea, or the *white glare* of the sun. Try and think of unusual ways to say these things.

9. **Endings**: If you set up a puzzle or conundrum or mystery about what's happening in your story, keep teasing the reader about how it's going to end. The story should move towards some kind of resolution, some kind of satisfaction of the plot that ties together the whole story. You can do this just as well with memoir as with fiction.

Exercise

Building a framework
Look again at the Mindmap you created in Chapter 3. It will have given you an idea of the main themes of the story.
Or make a storyboard (a large sheet of card and post it notes). Write a card/post-it

note for the beginning. Then the big events, dramatic moments.

What went wrong? How did you overcome these obstacles, what you did/didn't do? How was it all resolved?

Maybe you want to write a memoir about how you became a successful entrepreneur/ musician/ tapestry maker. Or how you moved from a fast-paced life in the city to setting up a successful olive-growing business on a Greek Island. Describe how you did it and the obstacles you overcame. Maybe your story focuses on one dramatic period of your life. Or it's a traveller's tale of a journey through the Far East or Africa. Again, what happened, how did you deal with all you encountered?

Who are you writing for, your target audience?

Chapter 13 Research

As part of the research for my first memoir, I travelled back to South Africa for the first time in twenty-nine years. Apartheid was gone. Fantastic of course. Yet everything had changed. But the land was the same wasn't it? Except, a rural area where we had lived on eight acres, near a pig farm, was now buried beneath a shanty town already more than a million people strong[16], called Khayelitsha – a township in the Western Cape, located on the Cape Flats near Cape Town. Crime and poverty, those two bedfellows, were rampant. Nelson Mandela was free, but was retired and in his late eighties.

It was 2007.It was a huge relief to be liberated from the appalling constraints of censorship and the secret police; to be able to go freely, to visit Robben Island, where Mandela had been incarcerated; and mourn for the way he was treated. It was lovely to enjoy this beautiful land without the fear of where you were

[16] Now (2017) 7 million.

and were not 'allowed' to go; to not be looking over your shoulder constantly and being careful what you could and could not speak about. And yet it felt like those constraints were still partly there, in my head at least. I would have to unpick them slowly to be free of them.

I headed for the Cape Town library near St George's Cathedral in town and read the newspapers for 1975-77. I hadn't trusted the information that was published in them at the time. Censorship meant the news was severely restricted – you had to read between the lines. We all knew about the men who were reported as having 'jumped' from the Security Headquarters, including the appalling tragedy of the murder of Steve Biko – he too had 'jumped' or so it was reported

The dilemma now became, should I write from the perspective of who I was then or should I write from my new perspective and knowledge, looking back?

I decided I'd choose the former. I'd use footnotes and quotations published in the Western press, unknown to the S African population due to censorship.

It felt important to write from my 'then' perspective with the reader somehow standing next to me, slightly behind, looking over my shoulder as an observer. It's all about Point of View (POV). If you write from later knowledge, your POV becomes what is called 'omniscient'. You've stepped out of the person you were then. Now you're 'god-like', looking down, with future knowledge.

No, no, no. Be very wary of doing that, you risk killing the immediacy of your story.

* * *

Do your research. Prepare it well. Here's a list of places to search/ find in that box in your attic/ at the back of your garage, in libraries, on Google, wherever.

- Old diaries (yours and other people's)
- Old newspapers (Go to libraries in the country where your story is set if you can or a connected website).
- Cards, tickets, programmes
- Photo albums – yours and other people's
- Other people's memories – this can be important for checking facts, but remember, their take on the facts will be subjective, different to yours. Ask them about people and circumstances, the clothes this person or that would wear, the car they drove, what did the front parlour look like?
- Other people's photo albums, programmes, souvenirs... Again these will serve as reminders for you. Often one small question will trigger your target person to talk and reminisce, as well as setting you off on strings of memories. Take notes or switch on your voice recorder (on your phone).
- They say using the internet for your research, is like sitting in the middle of a library and having thousands of books thrown at you. So be careful, wary and selective.
- Wikipedia is a great resource too, particularly for checking on someone well

known's details – birth, personal history, dates of tenure in office, age. Whether you're writing about the living or the dead – Wikipedia has the info. For example. you want to check the year David Bowie released Space Oddity, because that was the year a major drama unfolded in your life.

• Read other books or memoirs from the time and place of your story. This will give you background and context. It will also jog your memory about places, people and weather.

Give yourself time for reflection. Put all the bits of paper and notes in a folder for now. There's more planning to do.

Libraries are still a fantastic resource for books related to your topic – did you know that through the Inter-Library Loan service you can have any book in the UK system delivered to your local library. For America, check the American Library Association website for information.

Chapter 14 Libel, Slander and
Defamation

Defamation—also calumny, vilification, and traducement
—is the communication of a false statement that harms the
reputation of an individual person, business, product, group,
government, religion, or nation.
Under common law, to constitute defamation, a claim must
generally be false and must have been made to someone other
than the person defamed. Some common law jurisdictions also
distinguish between spoken defamation, called slander, and
defamation in other media such as printed words or images,
called libel.

http://en.wikipedia.co.uk/wiki/defamatio

Some of those I teach memoir writing to, are worried about defamation or libel. At the very least, they worry about upsetting people who they know or knew, who are part of their story.

I explain, that for defamation or libel to occur they would have to knowingly be telling untruths and the other person would have to prove that. If you relate back to **Chapter 2 – Truth is Stranger than Fiction**, I discussed how subjective truth is and sometimes how complicated.

There are many different ways to tell a story and truth is hard to define. The likelihood of someone suing you and succeeding in proving their case, is quite rare.

If you are clear that your story is true, if you're sure of the facts and you really want to tell the story, go ahead. Tell the story. Do it.

What if you're afraid that someone may not wish to be reminded of a particular event or events? You could think, well tough, that's the way it happened and I'm going to tell the story. Or you could just leave that part out or tone it down. Ask yourself, is it a crucial part of your story? If Yes - THEN TELL IT.

Another option is to change *your* name – give yourself a **nom de plume**. You can change a few of the details, which would make the story obvious and change the names of any characters in the book who you don't want to offend. Remember some people will be surprisingly pleased to be talked about in a book. Others, who you don't expect, will be angry or annoyed.

In my memoir, *A Hippopotamus at the Table*, I changed the names of quite a few people who I thought might be unhappy, as I was talking about events that had been sad or upsetting for them.

One person, a key character, has not spoken to me since the book was published – not because they read it, the person refuses to read the book. Maybe, (I can only surmise), the book talked about a period of time and series of events that the person did not want to think about again.

But these events were equally difficult and traumatic for me, I also lived through them. Should this have stopped *me* from telling my story?

This quote is from Stephen King in his book:

On Writing: A Memoir of the Craft.

'If you want to succeed as a writer, rudeness should be the second-to-least of your concerns. The least of all should be polite society and what it expects. If you intend to write as truthfully as you can, your days as a member of polite society, are numbered anyway.'

And he was talking about fiction writing! This quote is cheering. Memoir writing is a hard road, you have to have a strong calling. You have to believe you have a story to tell, perhaps a burning story you have lived through, something quite unique, that you want to tell from your perspective.

If your story needs to be told, you really want to, then tell it. Don't wait for permission (who from for goodness sake?). Give yourself permission. You have to – no one else cares unless they have their own vested interest in YOUR story   As long as you are telling your own story of things, events that happened to you, that you observed and want to tell people about, I say again WRITE IT!

Exercise

Make a list of five key characters in your story. Number them 1-5. Write a sentence or two, about how each of these five played their part in your story, for good or bad.

Is there anything you want to write about them that is untrue or false? I doubt it. You are writing your memoir to tell about events and things that happened, that are true from your perspective. That's all you need to concentrate on. You can't generally be libelous therefore.

If you're still worrying, change your name and change their name in the story, from Bill to Dave or whatever. Choose an author name, a nom-de-plume, have some fun with it. Write it down and practise saying it out loud … Preston Houdini, Jasmine Botticelli or whoever, then say 'author.' Sounds good yes?

Chapter 15 Copyright and plagiarism

What does it mean for you and your book?

> Legal definition of copyright: *the exclusive and assignable legal right, given to the originator for a fixed number of years to print, publish, perform, film or record literary or artistic materials.*
> UK Copyright Office - www.copyright.co.uk

You might think it fair or reasonable for you to copy chunks of other people's writing, pictures, screen-shots and use it in your writing projects, books, etc. But in that case, is it fair and reasonable for others to do the same with your writing material?

When I first started out as a poet, being ignorant of copyright law and thinking someone might want to plagiarise my poems, I used to put the small © copyright symbol at the end of every poem. Nowadays, I don't bother – why?

Because everything you write is automatically copyrighted as soon as you write it.

When you publish your book, you (or your publisher) put a legal reminder near the beginning in what's called the 'Front Matter' of your book (Front Matter is the pages before the Contents or before the start of Chapter 1).

On the page after the title, you put the copyright wording, together with the name of the publishers (if you have one) and year of first publication. The copyright statement is to remind people of your rights to your own material – here's the one from my memoir book, 'A *Hippopotamus at the Table*'– I just changed the names. Feel free to copy the wording for your Front Matter if you want to.

Mustard Seed Press

Once your book is published, you have formalised your copyright. But even before that, your material is your own and copyrighted.

There is one *however*, I would add in this age of the internet. In theory you are protected across the world, in every country (although laws vary somewhat from country to country). But, if someone far away gets access to and plagiarises your Opus Magnus and they live in a country where laws are not the same or are not enforced – are you going to afford to hire an international lawyer to track them down and sue them? Oprah Winfrey might… just saying. Be careful where you upload your book to, and ensure you have a good firewall on your laptop or computer.

Don't let this make you paranoid however. The chances of anyone else plagiarising your story are remote. These are just sensible basic precautions.

What it means for you - using, quoting or copying the work of others?

What's the protocol? It seems to be fairly flexible if you want to copy a few lines or even a few paragraphs of prose from someone's work. Generally, no one is going to bother about that as long as you acknowledge your source. It does depend on the length and purpose of the quotation. There's a useful guide in a publication from the Society of Authors.[17]

If you quote an author – famous or

[17] **https://tinyurl.com/y88ea75j**

otherwise, you'd reference their full name and also the title of the book or publication, where the quote/extract is from. Then add the year of publication, or alternatively the web address will do. Finally we generally put the name of the publishing company.

Similarly, if you quote from an article on a website or online, you should acknowledge where it came from, by providing the web address of the source, year of publication and author name.

How long does copyright last after the death of the author?

That depends on the country. In the EU for example the copyright term was extended from 50 years to 70 years after the death of the author. In some countries it might be 25 or 35 years. *[Wikipedia.org]*

Music Copyright

This is a whole different ball game. Music copyright laws are much more complicated. Music and lyrics written since 1923 are NOT in the public domain.

Music companies vigorously defend their rights - damages might be claimed or worse still you'll be forced to shred every copy of your book. [No really, not just the bit where you use the lyrics … All of it]. If you do quote from a song, prepare for a lawyer's letter or a lawsuit. *You cannot copy song lyrics without permission*.

When I have wanted to quote lines from song lyrics, copyright is such a minefield, that I have mainly decided not to. You can paraphrase general lyrics and use the title. That's it.

If you really want to go ahead and quote lines from lyrics, here's what you do. First find the songwriter/ publisher. The publisher of all well-known musicians, owns and manages the copyright. It can take ages to track them down – they might be an American company.

Then you write to them and they MIGHT say 'OK, go ahead and we won't charge you,' (not very likely). Or they'll say 'Yes' and quote you a big fat fee, usually hundreds of pounds/dollars.

Therefore, quote the song title and *paraphrase* a line or two of lyrics, or if you can be creative, make up a song. Make up lyrics that capture the mood you want to create. You can also write to the Hal Leonard Corporation or Alfred Music Publishing, quoting song title, publisher, publication date and giving the excerpt you want to use. Include (if you can find out) the territory of distribution. They should be able to direct you to the publisher of the song, who can give you a quote on cost.

Articles to read:

Look up - Bookbaby *'How to Legally Quote Song Lyrics in your Book.'*[18] It basically says what I've said above. Or you can read *Can I Use Song Lyrics in my Manuscript?* WritersDigest.com.[19]

* * *

Plagiarism

Oxford Dictionary definition: *The practise of taking someone else's work and passing it off as your own.*

Webster*: to steal and pass off (the ideas*

---

[18] **http://blog.bookbaby.com/2013/10/lyrics-in-books/**
[19] **https://tinyurl.com/y9b6fvgf**

and words of another) as one's own without crediting the source.

Different then to copyright.

'.. Where copyright infringement is a construct of the law, plagiarism is a construct of ethics.' [20]

When I was teaching at a London college, an essay was handed in to me by someone whose first language was not English, someone who's spoken English I knew to be between basic and intermediate. The entire essay was in perfect 1950s English. . .

I called him in and told him that I was not able to accept his essay and that the college took a dim view of plagiarism. In fact, in most universities it is a matter for immediate expulsion from the college. I decided to give him another opportunity to write the essay himself.

I never did get another essay from him and soon after I believe he dropped out of the course. Presumably, he'd paid someone else (someone educated in the 1950s) to write the essay for him and tried to pass the essay off as his own. This is fraud.

However if you, as a writer, pay someone else to write a book or even just a chapter for you in your book, is that fraud /plagiarism also? You are not trying to get a college degree in that case or breaking the rules of a University.

---

[20] **www.plagiarismtoday.com/2013/10/07/difference-copyright**

It's a tricky subject, as the line between the two is often thin. But generally, as long as you acknowledge the writer's input into your book somewhere, it's fine – maybe as a footnote or endnote or in your acknowledgement page at the beginning of the book.

Chapter 16 Editing and Reviewing

When you get to the point where you're ready to edit/review your book, it's an exciting moment. I remember writing '**The End**' when I'd finally finished writing the last chapter. For a long time, I'd dreaded that last chapter. How would I end the story? I knew where it ended, it was a memoir, not a novel. It ended with us leaving South Africa and returning to London. But bringing the story all together to that point and rounding up loose ends, that was going to be a challenge.

I finally decided that the farewell party we'd had in that Cape Town, November (summer), for all our friends, would be the perfect vehicle for describing our last days there. And because it was a party, I thought of all the music that was played and how the music formed the backdrop for my interactions with the many people we'd met there. I made a list of all the music tracks that I could remember – I also realised that those tracks gave the party context, time and setting. The one that stood out was an album we'd acquired a few months before. It had come out that year (1977) – Brian Ferry and Roxy Music. I listened to it again and I was there, right there again, watching the party unfold.

I decided to call the final chapter after one of the iconic songs - 'This is Tomorrow Calling.' It symbolised the end of one era and our turning towards a different future. That's how I got to MY ending. How are you going to get to YOUR ending? What symbols will you use?

You might think that now the hard work is done. It's just a short time until you'll be holding that book in your hands. Wrong. Wrong. Wrong. I hope not to put you off, but the editing process is the beginning of a lot more hard work.

I read through my book about 50 times (over the course of writing and re-writing it, in a two-year period), making changes and corrections. I was so sick of the book by the time it was anywhere near a publishable manuscript. I'm not just talking about spelling and grammar either. There's so much more than that.

I had very little idea of what was involved in editing beforehand. Let's go through some of the steps.

Firstly read it through from the beginning to the end in one sitting (if you can). Listen to how it flows and how the themes work. Can you identify the overall main theme of the book? Without themes and how they flow through the story, your book's a string of events or anecdotes. The theme is not the plot of the story. Themes can be redemption, alienation, betrayal, courage, isolation, loss, love, power, prejudice, spirituality, growing up, becoming aware and many more. Think about your story. Maybe, through writing your story, the themes have come to light, become visible. My story touched on quite a few themes from that list, plus some unique to my story.

Editing Steps

• Self-editing
Before you think about showing your precious book to anyone, first it's spelling and grammar checking. If, like me you've written around 100,000 words, the editing takes weeks. Things to check -

• **Repetition** - have you described things in one chapter and further along you've described the same thing again? Repetition also involves using the same adjective or adverb in the same paragraph or even page. Use your Thesaurus, be creative.

• **Writing Style** - Have you used fancy complicated words in a description, when simpler words sound better? Have you used over-colourful phrases or sentences, which need to be toned down?

• Editing Tips
• Check your sentence lengths. Long rambling sentences don't work. Cut them up.

• Check your dialogue – each line of new speech must start with a single quote mark (Americans tend to use double quotes and so do some (*old-fashioned?*) English writers). Check that each beginning and end line of dialogue has a quote mark. Make sure the start of any dialogue is on a new line. At the end of your spoken line, always put full stops and commas **INSIDE** the quote marks - e.g.

'*Go home,*' he said, '*there's nothing more to do today.*'

'*Have you got a light?*' She leant forward and held back her long sweep of blonde hair, as he clicked his lighter. '*Thanks.*' She took a long slow drag and exhaled a smoke ring, tilting her face up.

Notice where each quote mark comes – **outside** other punctuation....usually ... remember English is full of exceptions and anomalies.

• Make sure you put in commas, separating different thoughts, so that the sentence meaning is clear. Conversely, don't put in too many commas or put them in the wrong places.

• Rarely use exclamation marks – that is a sign of poor writing.

• Don't do the dreaded 'of' instead of 'have', that so many new writers in their 20s and 30s do today. 'Of' is not a verb, it is not the same as '*has*' or '*have*'. Every time I see 'of' used this way I shudder. 'He should **of** gone home,' for he should **have** gone home – unless you're doing dialogue appropriate to the speaker i.e. in quotes.

• Remove increased (i.e. double or 1.5) line spacing if you are formatting for a book (Home/Paragraph/Spacing – "0" "0" single).

Make sure there's no spacing between paragraphs. Just use one millimetre indentation on a line, to show the start of each new paragraph. This will decide the number of pages you have in your book. The more pages, the higher the printing costs.

• Remember that the average paperback size is c. 8 x 5.5. If you're writing your book in Word, format it to that size (Page Layout/Size). It gives you an idea of the number of pages. But it will need to be put into a book template (eg. on Amazon KDP). Think about holding a book open in the middle. You'll notice the left page has a larger margin on the right. The right page has a larger margin on the left. That's why you need the template.

When you've done all that, you've got to the point where you can't bear to go through the book *again* especially if you're a perfectionist like me. Move on. Remember it'll NEVER be perfect – YOU HAVE TO LET GO AND GIVE IT UP FOR THE NEXT PHASE **OR YOU'LL NEVER PUBLISH**. It's time to let other people read it (scary).

Now, have you got a few people who will look through it for you and give you feedback? They need to be people with reasonable literary skills or at least people who read a lot, who you can trust (I mean (a) trust to tell you the truth and not flatter you and (b) trust to give constructive, not crushing, criticism.) If you don't have anyone like that in your circles, then use writer/author websites (for example, Authors Unite). You can usually post up at least part of your story and ask for some feedback.

Be specific about what you want. Give a list of questions – for instance, does the story flow, hang together and does the first chapter encourage them to read on? Do the chapters link well together? What do they think of the ending? Is the overall spelling and grammar OK? DON'T ask for a complete edit. You'll need to do that yourself or pay someone to do it for you. It's a big task.

Finding an editor. There are several kinds of editing that you can pay for. There's developmental editing, copy editing, proof reading. Each has a price tag. Do some online research or ask in one of the writer's websites/forums for help in finding one that has a recommended track record and who's within your budget. Then it's a question of putting it out to tender for some quotes. You must be prepared to pay from £400-£600 for a basic editing job on a 100,000 word book. If you have the money and want a top-notch job you can pay £1000 upwards. Some editors charge by number of words, some by pages and some by the hour.

If you get a writer's agent to take you on, of course they will organise this for you.

1)   **Developmental editing** involves evaluating the whole book for content, structure, flow. This form of editing is completely thorough and involves a great deal of in depth work by the editor.

2)   **Copy editing**
This type of editing focuses on grammar, style, repetition, word usage.

3)   **Proof reading** – involves spelling, punctuation, grammar and style.

Things to watch out for – you need to find an editor who you can get on with. You must be confident that he/she won't leave you wanting to give up and put the book in a bottom drawer and forget about it forever. That happened to me with one editor who I paid for. I didn't pick up the book again for two years, after this person's feedback. My small bit of confidence evaporated, because there was so much critical commentary and not enough encouragement.

However, when I picked it up two years later (my dogged determination kicked in again eventually), it was all so useful and helped improve the book enormously. Reading again through the critiques, chapter by chapter, I realised that most of it was right. I rewrote many chapters, improved the flow of the story and made some of the themes (eg. racial conflict) much stronger, with new chapters. It's difficult, but you do need to develop a thick skin, if you want that essential feedback. That's hard for creative people.

After you've recovered from the editing process, (I hope it doesn't take *you* two years) and looked at the advice and feedback from friends and relatives, it's time to do the rewrites. This involves accepting or rejecting the suggestions and changes. **You** make the final decisions and **you** talk to the editor about their suggestions that you want to query. Finally, do you want them to go through it again? That's called an '*editing pass*' and you'll be charged for it. Or you might just decide to do it for yourself, if you have a limited budget.

When your final edited draft is ready, you pay your editor (if you've got one). If you feel they've done a good job, give them a good review and/or a recommendation.

If you have a publishing deal with a traditional publishing house, then of course you pay nothing. It's all part of the contract. If you are self-publishing you do. It's either pay for separate services yourself (eg, editing, publishing, marketing) or you do it all yourself, using authors websites and Amazon DIY books to study how to do it all.

Are you ready for the next scary and exciting bit? I mean publishing your book!

Chapter 17 Traditional Publishing

"Authors need to bring the same level of rigour to evaluating their publishing options as publishers bring to evaluating manuscripts. If you don't hold the tiller, someone else will grab it." Eliot Peper[21]

Getting published the traditional way

The traditional way to get published is with a conventional big publisher. The main ones are –
Penguin Random House, Hachette Livre, Harper Collins, Pan MacMillan, Pearson Education, Oxford University Press (OUP), Bloomsbury, Simon and Schuster. Some of these are umbrella publishers for a list of other smaller publishers. For example Random House has Chatto & Windrus, Jonathan Cape, and Bodley Head etc. Hachette Livre includes Hodder & Stoughton, Sceptre, Quercus and quite a few others.

---

[21] Publishing With a Small Press: Straddling the Indie-Traditional Gap. Eliot Peper March 2015

1. **Getting an agent**

Most of these can only be approached via **an agent.** First therefore, you have the agent hurdle. Am I making that sound like an obstacle course? Well that's because it is.

Subscribe to **Agent Hunter** (not expensive) or buy **The Creative Writing Handbook** – latest version (or a second-hand version from Amazon) or read it in the library. There are various resources to get an accurate, up-to-date list of agents. **Agent Hunter**, [**www.agenthunter.co.uk**], is Harry Bingham's website - he's a best-selling crime writer. This site lists each agent in the UK, together with brief info about them, what genre they publish, links to their websites and also their submissions policies. Each agent is different, some big, some small and you improve your chance of success by reading these submissions policies carefully.

Therefore, if an agent states that they don't accept email submissions – then don't waste your time. If they say they only accept fiction – don't send them a memoir/non-fiction manuscript. If they say send the first 3 chapters of your MS, then don't send the whole book. Agent Hunter also explains how to write a *pitch letter* (how to sell yourself to an agent]. You can also get good instruction on writing a pitch letter in **Mslexia** (a women writer's magazine, but you don't have to be female to look). Those are the resources I know and have used. Other sites include

- **www.writersdigest.com/edior-blogs**.

- **https://mybookeditors.com**

- **www.writersworkshop.co.uk**

All of these have good instructions about how to write a letter to an agent and how to enquire whether they might be interested in representing you.

Before you start there's a few things to bear in mind:

Agents (and publishers) generally do not want to look at your memoir unless it is a finished manuscript with good quality writing, although some may be happy to give advice on improvements.

It should be original, not just your own work (that's obvious) but also a story that is unusual in some way - that doesn't mean weird and full of unsubstantiated conspiracy theories. Preferably, a story that no one else has told, written in a way that is different and has a strong 'voice'. It should have the potential to become, a page turner/ best seller, not just in the UK, but also on the European and Worldwide stage. Either that or it will sell to a good size 'niche' market, like Chick Lit (Bridget Jones), 'Misery 'Lit, Travel Lit, Celebrity Lit, action, drama, spiritual, romance, humour etc.

Now, before you pick up your manuscript and chuck it in the bottom drawer of a remote cupboard on the top landing, sobbing quietly, STOP.

First of all you're probably a newby writer and so you either have too much confidence to the point of narcissism about your opus magnus, *or* your confidence levels bounce along the bottom of the pond amongst the mud, detritus, newts and tadpoles.

If you're the former, just bring your fantasies down to reality level. Perhaps not everyone will share your very high opinion about the beauty and genius of your writing.

If you're the latter - self-flagellating/ my-work-is-rubbish, no one will like it or like me – just start doing some positive self-talk.

Or perhaps you bounce between the two…?

Time to give yourself a firm mental shake. Lift up your head and think about how much joy (as well as stress and hard work) your writing gives you. Think about how much life experience you have and what a story you have to tell. It's unique and it's your story. It belongs to you.

In either case, if you haven't completed years of writing groups and creative writing courses, to improve your writing skills - it's time you started. Go find a course or writing group. Hone your skills. Do short courses or a degree course (try Open University for example. It's online, in your own time). Do you have experience in a different kind of writing – journalism, report writing? Have you had feedback from other writers, literary friends? Another important way to improve your writing skills is by reading lots of other memoir writers, going to writing classes and receiving feedback. Just get clear about your vision – which is to get published. There it is in the bookshop window – your title and your name on the cover. Wow. Hold on to that thought.

We've discussed sites where you can look for an agent. Next send out [perhaps 5?] letters at a time, your pitch letter, plus a sample of your work.

Each agent you pick will have been carefully checked by you, to see that they accept memoirs, cold call submissions and how they want to be approached.

Now I'm going to paint you a rather depressing picture, the reality of what happens in a *big* agents' office. So I advise you to hum a little 'keep your spirits up' tune in your head – like Winnie-the-Pooh does in that book '*The Hums of Pooh*'. Of course, what I'm saying may be different in a *small* agent's office.

Picture one of those offices, where you have chosen to send your pitch letter and 3 chapters. A junior clerical assistant has picked up your manuscript from a pile on their desk [this pile is the one they call the 'slush pile']. He/she is glancing through your letter and if that passes, or something catches their eye in this brief scan, they might glance through the first page of your manuscript. He or she has at least 50 manuscripts, being sent to the agency every week, to go through.

If your letter is badly written, grammar not good, manuscript page1 has typos and a fancy font, together with poor formatting - see that large bin in the corner near her desk? Yep, probably about 45 of those manuscripts in the pile on his/her desk will end up there. Or maybe they'll get a standard 'Dear Jill/John letter', with a two line rejection.

If you're lucky, you'll be in that small pile in the corner of her/his desk that will be passed on to the actual agent. This means only that grammar and typos are OK, formatting is passable *and* the subject area fits the agency's current focus of attention.

The subject area or criteria for inclusion by the way will be narrow – it *is* for fiction. Memoir as a subject area is VERY NARROW. Your book does not need to be in a unique bracket all its own. Quite the contrary. More often it needs to be in a reasonably popular category, unless it's a unique work of creative genius. It should cover an angle no one else is covering within that category.

So if it's 'misery-lit' it must be DIFFERENT misery-lit. If it's a *'redemption'* story (how you conquered abuse, addiction, whatever) and came out the wonderful whole human you became as a result), then it must have a unique angle somewhere. Think Bob the Cat. So probably stories that focus on *how my cat saved me from a life on drugs* will not be accepted – it's been done … and it's been turned into a movie. Next.

Or if it's a travel saga - your gap year in Thailand stories need to have a unique angle to make them stand out from all the others – Phuket in the Tsunami anyone? I know – poor taste, but you get my drift. And that would likely end up being a redemption story anyway, For example - my best friend saved me from drowning or something. I digress -

Back to publishers, the Biggies. If you get an agent and if your agent sells your book to a big publisher then you would get (OMG magic!) perhaps, what feels like a big advance - $5000? $10,000? Or whatever equivalent currency you have in your country. The money is NOT for you to pay off all your credit cards (although you could). It's so you can take time out to write the book, up to the standard they want.

Which of course sounds fabulous – you think you'll write better if you lock yourself away on a tiny island or in a remote country cottage? Maybe some people would, but I know I would do zero writing somewhere remote. Nada, zilch. I like libraries, beach cafes, places where I'm undisturbed but amongst people.

Last week, I was heartened, listening to an interview with JK Rowling, that she feels the same. When she was writing all the Harry Potter books she always felt oppressed with the silence, if she was alone at home. She had to go out and write in cafes, somewhere where there were people about. I'm not the only one then.

Step 2. Go straight to a Publisher (miss out *'finding an agent'* which was Step 1).

You can of course (did you know?) pitch your story/ manuscript / book straight to a publisher. Some publishers accept submissions without the middle-woman/man. Do some research and check out their submission guidelines. There's an Online American authors' magazine you can subscribe to called 'Author Publish Magazine'. It does some listings with the UK market but generally not the big publishers. It sends you lists of different small publishers who are looking for submissions. And it pays authors/writers to write articles for the magazine, articles for other writers. Which brings me to my next category of publisher.

A.   Small Publishers

Many of these are run by interested, experienced, enthusiasts (some of whom have broken away from the Biggies to set up their own publishing companies), who want to support writers on their journey to get published. They'll give you proper, constructive feedback about your writing.

If you fail to get the attention of the Major Publishers, this is an option. They'll tell you if you need to work on your writing skills. They are also, unlike the Big Publishers who are more commercially driven, more willing to take a risk on you, if they see talent and artistic merit. Be warned though, they will not be interested in you unless they know you're in a saleable bracket. Another big plus with small presses is that they accept direct submissions without an agent.

Because they're small, they don't have large amounts of capital to fall back on. However, they're more hands on, you'll get time and attention and you can build a good relationship with the owner/ editor/designer. And they're more likely to see marketing your book as a long-term project, rather than as a short sprint and then no more.

Advances from small publishers are small **up to** £10,000, some less - (unlike the much bigger payouts from the Big Five). But remember all payouts are paid against royalties – that's how they earn their money, out of the profits. From a big Publishing House you'll get c, 5-15% royalties for print books and 25% for e-book sales. With a small press you can get a much higher percentage of your royalties.

However, although you'll get advice and some help with publicity and marketing, your input will be required to be much higher with the marketing (than with a big publishing house). You'll be expected to organise a lot of your own publicity, touring bookstores, organising book signings and building mailing lists via your website/blog. *"Creativity does not end with writing the book."*[22]

This option is easier than *self-publishing* as the publisher knows the process and gives you advice on the quality of your writing.

* * *

[22] Publishing with a Small Publisher. Robert Lee Brewer. April 2014
Publishing with a Small Press. Jane Friedman. March 2015

Many writers still prefer to hand over their work to a traditional publisher and let them do everything.

Financially it's a good option, as the publisher is putting up the capital and taking all the risks on selling your work.

If your book does become a best-seller, they take all the profits to compensate for their initial financial outlay. Your book will be placed in all the best book-selling outlets all over the country, bookshops, airports, supermarkets. The traditional publisher has to recoup their outlay.

The down side is that if your book doesn't sell, it'll be off the shelves and dumped really fast, within a few months. They will own the rights to your book so you *can't* go out and sell it yourself. It will probably be a number of years before you can get the rights back to your book.

B. Vanity Presses.

If you find a small publisher who tells you your book is marvelous, heaps on the flattery, but quotes you a very large fee for all the things that need doing to make it publishable, editing, marketing, book cover design. It's time for you to do some independent research into the name of the company on Google… you may find plaintive authors talking about how much they've put in and got very little in return, hardly any book sales and the company doesn't seem to be answering their emails or they're making loads of excuses about 'the market' for your type of book.

These are vanity presses – they flatter and cajole you out of large sums of money for a finished product of variable quality, just so you can sell to friends and family. No one else will buy them. They will not tell you the truth about your writing. They will not tell you to go away and spend 2-5 years improving your writing and getting your manuscript up to scratch. They will not direct you to writing courses and so on, so you can learn how to become a better writer. Of course they won't. They want your money NOW.

There are many of these 'vanity' presses out there. These vanity presses are NOT self-publishing and they are often confused with it. They give self-publishing a bad name. Be clear it is NOT the same thing. The problem is that those who support the agent/ big publisher route often denigrate self-publishing as if it's the same as vanity press. It's not. We're coming to more on the subject of self-publishing further on.

Rejection letters

Check out these excerpts from REAL famous author rejections:

1. Sylvia Plath: There certainly isn't enough genuine talent for us to take notice.

2. Rudyard Kipling: I'm sorry Mr Kipling, but you just don't know how to use the English language.

3. J.G. Ballard: The author of this book is beyond psychiatric help.

4. Emily Dickinson: [Your poems] are quite as remarkable for defects as for beauties and are generally devoid of true poetical qualities

5. Ernest Hemingway (regarding The Torrents of Spring): It would be extremely rotten taste, to say nothing of being horribly cruel, should we want to publish it.

6. The first Harry Potter book by JK Rowling was turned down 12 times. Her first detective crime novel, sent off in the name of Robert Galbraith, Cuckoo's Calling, she was told 'could not [be published] with commercial success.'

Say no more really. Some give you encouraging feedback. Some don't. Some are right. Some are wrong.

* * *

Chapter 18 Self-Publishing

The more I explored the publishing options for this book, the more I realised that self-publishing has now become such a large subject, that it needed, not the little sub-section I was going to give it, but a chapter all its own.

The actual self-publishing process is relatively easy. There are various options. Do you want to publish a print book or an e-book? Or both? There are some platforms that make it really simple. View the top twenty platforms on **http://www.bookrunch.com/top/selfpublish/**.

And don't look down your nose at self-publishing or let other people do so either. The digital revolution has changed the face of publishing forever. Think about it and read this article – there's a link in the footnote.

'*It seems The Honeypot of Self-Publishing is getting sweeter and sweeter by the day for the publishing industry. The appearance of just one self-published book on the **New York Times Bestseller list** would have raised quite a few eyebrows not too many years ago, and, yet, just* *a few weeks ago (**Aug 5th**), no less than seven titles by four different authors graced the list. Of course, we are talking about the New York Times e-book fiction list, but nonetheless it reflects how times have changed.[23]*

The same article also goes on to say *'The borders between legacy [traditional publishing] and self-publishing are constantly blurring. As each year goes by, more publishers are developing self-publishing imprints, and, interestingly, we are also seeing a number of companies offering self-publishing services across the divide ....*

*It is very clear that the largest global company offering self-publishing **services** to authors—**Author Solutions Inc, now a Penguin company**—has played a big hand, over the past three years in promoting its resources to publishers as well as authors.'*

That article was written in 2012 – things have moved on rapidly since then.

Emily Benet[24], a writer who emerged in the last few years, got published the traditional way with her first and second novels. Here's what she has to say about the experience -

'… the big publisher did minimal marketing and low royalties meant that two years of work for two books barely earned me enough to pay a month's rent.

---

[23]
http://www.theindependentpublishingmagazine.com/2012/09/the-self-publishing-honeypot.html Mick Rooney. The Honey Pot of Self-Publishing,
[24] http://emilybenet.blogspot.co.uk/

*Insanity is doing the same thing over and over and expecting different results... So this summer I published **The Hen Party** under my own brand **Little Cactus**. To date the book has sold more in three months than my traditionally published books did in a year.'*

For Emily her childhood dream was to get an agent and be published the traditional way *'in the end this dream really was a huge disappointment that has taken me a while to come to terms with.'*

You CAN self-publish now without the old stigma, you don't have to do all the work yourself and you can make money from your book sales.

If you want a really good finished product you can do some of the tasks yourself and then depending on your financial resources and skill-set, you can buy in some of the services so you come out with a professional looking imprint/ book.

Some of these include professional editing, formatting your manuscript for the e-book market, creating a book cover, marketing and publicity. Big publishing companies are now recognising the market for these services and hiring out some of them through smaller sub-companies – like Author Solutions (Penguin).

Here's some *how-to books* about self-publishing that you can get on Kindle or in print –

13 Million Reasons Why Self-Publishing Rocks, by HM Ward;
Self-Publishing Books 101, Shelley Hitz.

To Self-publish or Not to Self-publish: A Seriously Useful Author's Guide, by Mick Rooney. (Well written)

There's another Self-Publishing guide (Free) at Author House – here's the link: **www.authorhouse.co.uk/self-publish /free_guide**. I'm not endorsing any of these – you must look and decide what's useful yourself. I've read some, not all. Quality varies.

There's many sites that can help you on your self-publishing path – Google search 'Self-publishing' and you'll get a long list. How you publish depends what input you want into the process, how good you want your book to appear and what is your budget. My budget was always close to zero, so I tried to learn how to do as much as I could myself. I'll explain how you can do the same – but it's your choice – pick and choose.

I'll tell you about a few of the main platforms:

Self-Publishing Options –

1.   Lulu [https://www.lulu.com]

Lulu is a tried and tested self-publishing website and has been around for years. If you're totally computer-illiterate (even if you're not quite that bad) it's the easiest option. They have a good basic *how to* section which describes the processes involved.

•   Choose your book size and colour – usually black on white for interior and colour for cover, paperback size about

8 x 4-5 inches – the site will explain.

- You just upload your completely ready, well-edited and checked Word file (your manuscript/book) and the platform does most of it for you including helping you create a cover. They give you a large range of covers to choose from and a wizard takes you through the process. But the covers are often fairly basic to look at.

2. KDP Kindle Direct Publishing

This is a website for uploading and publishing your book onto Kindle, an Amazon platform. Take a look, you just follow the steps. [http://www.kdp.amazon.com/].

This platform is relatively easy to use, but more hands on than Lulu. Good for print books. It works like this.

- Prepare and edit your *'Interior matter'* - your book or manuscript from Chapter 1 onwards. Follow the instructions in my Chapter 16 – *Editing and Reviewing.*

- Open an **Amazon KDP** account (it's free). Follow the instructions for uploading your file. You can upload it as a Word doc or as a pdf – it used to be just pdf. You can save and convert any Word file as a 'pdf'. Got to File/Save/Export.

This is a basic guide, but if you want a more in-depth list of instructions, there are several books on Amazon you can download for a low price. These will take you through the baby-steps – eg. **Amazon KDP and Kindle, Self-Publishing Masterclass**, by Rick Smith*; Self-Publishing Tips for Amazon KDP Authors*, by Glyn Williams; Search **Amazon** for more if you like.

Also the Amazon KDP website itself has a good guide.

If you decide to use Amazon KDP, here's the steps.

a.   You've opened an account and are logged in. You'll see a list of options:

b.   Click on *Title* – put in the main title name, then subtitle, then author name(s). For example:

- Title :*My Memoir*

- Subtitle *: A Story from My Life*

- Author Name: *Jane/Jim Author*

c.   Next click *Interior*. Upload your Word document from whichever drive you've stored it on -. desktop, **usb** stick, external hard drive, iCloud. The file should be ready formatted in a consistent and 'clean' style. Before Chapter 1 it should include around 5 pages of *Front Matter*

(a) title page,

(b) blank page,

(c) Copyright stuff (copy from above p74).

(d) Forward page –if you want one

(e) Acknowledgements Page

(f) Address the Reader page, about reviews, your other publications, link to your website.

(g) Contents table with Chapter headings – each chapter heading on the list linked directly to the actual chapter [create a Table of Contents in Word – go to References/Table of Contents.

(h) Your main manuscript/content/story.

d.   Next go to '**cover**' and upload your cover file. It should be a **.jpg** picture file.

OK let's pause there – you *have* got a cover prepared yes? A proper cover with front and back pages laid out with a spine in the middle, together with artwork and text? If not, save what you've done on **Amazon KDP** so far, for later. I'll tell you options for creating a cover further down.

3.   Smashwords

This site is for e-Book sales sites in general, but not Kindle. If you use **KDP** you can choose one of two options – to tie up exclusively with KDP and receive 70% royalties – then you don't sell to other e-book platforms. Or you choose a non-exclusive deal and receive 30% royalties, which means you can sell your book on Kobo, ePub, Bookeen and other eBook platforms. The KDP Select deal binds you to only Kindle sales for an initial period, that's if you want the 70% royalties deal.

PREPARING A COVER My first advice would be to open **Amazon** or one of the other bookselling websites. Or perhaps GoodReads. Look carefully at the book covers. Remember that the publicity window on Amazon for your book will only have a **thumbnail size picture** of your cover. It's essential that the name and title stand out against the background so when it's reduced to thumbnail size you can still see it. It's the first thing people will look at, and most people's attention span, given the amount of material we are all looking at every day, is that of a gnat. So your cover has to catch their attention in that brief nano-second when their glance slides over it. It has to be easily readable.

You've got three options:

(i)   Get someone else to make you a cover or

(ii)   Create your own.

(iii)   Choose a generic design from a website like Lulu, which does it all for you via a wizard and hundreds of pictures from its picture bank.

A.   **Get someone else to do it**

Go to a website like **Fiverr** and commission someone else to create your cover for $5 (in theory). Actually it's more like $15-$40 per cover. Either get them to choose a picture for the cover or send one of your own (there are sites that let you use their pictures for free, or use one of your own photographs. Otherwise you will have to obtain permission and pay for using the picture. . It's so cheap you can commission say 2 or 3 of them and then choose the best. I wasn't *that* impressed when I tried it for this book. The cover ideas were a bit obvious and tacky, I felt. But I did get some ideas for how the cover could look. Cost me about $15 each for an Amazon thumbnail pic (that's not the whole cover, which you only need for print books).

B.   Or *if* you can pay a bit more go to *www.coverdesignstudio.com*

They have a huge library of book cover templates to choose from. If your book is only for Kindle/ e-books you just need a front cover, it'll cost around $30. If it's for a print book, you'll need a front cover, spine and back cover design. Cost will be about $45.

C.   Go to a website like **Upwork** - *__https://www.upwork.com__* or **Freelancer** - *www.freelancer.com.*

They are 'hiring' sites –you pay them an hourly rate about $5-$12(?). The sites are annoying as they make you sign up and tell them the project first before giving you a price, but hey. Ask the designer (based probably in Eastern Europe or India where wages are low) to send thumbnail samples of their work. You can offer a 2-hour fee for 3 ideas. Or ask a few of them to submit designs. When you've chosen one, order a **Kindle** version and a **KDP** full cover version. State that the copyright is yours and offer (if you want a really good job done) 4-5 hours pay.

a.   Or you can pay much more from about $75-$250- $500 to commission a designer to work on your cover. Check out this link - https://99designs.com/book-cover-design. **Or top end $750-$5000 -** http://bookdesigners.com/

b.   Kindle (KDP) offer their own online cover design options for free – choose *Build Your Cover Online* and you can launch *Cover Creator*, which puts in the title and subtitle and author name for you. Your back cover material can be copied and pasted in. For beginners it's easy to use and does it quickly. It will also insert the **Amazon KDP** free **ISBN** and barcode on the back cover (bottom right), if that's what you want and you haven't got one of your own.

4.   Design Your Own Cover or DIY.

Lots more work and your time of course. Only choose this option if you have some reasonable basic art skills. It takes a lot more time, but it's quite fun if you enjoy doing something 'arty'. You do need an artistic 'eye'. I had some help from my cousin who's an artist. I knew what I wanted, I just needed her to fine-tune my idea in Photoshop. Here's how to do it yourself:

(i)   Find a photograph that you like that relates to your content. It has to be 300 *dpi* – I'll explain - that's the number of pixels (dots) used to make up the picture – 300 dpi plus is sufficient quality for your cover. Nowadays, you can go to a website called **https://convert.town/image-dpi**. This site ups the *dpi* for you easily and quickly – just open your image, copy it, drag it to their box, drop it in. Make sure it says it'll convert your pic to 300+dpi. Resave it eg. newbookcoverpic in *jpeg.* Next you've got a few options:

(ii)   You can use **Photoshop** (complicated without training);

(iii)   Follow the instructions on **You Tube** to '**Design a Book Cove**r';

(iv)   Use **Microsoft Publisher** – much simpler than Photoshop;

(v)   Use the **Amazon KDP** template. When it's done, save and load the pdf into Publisher. The templates will include front cover, spine and back cover.

(vi) If you're using **Microsoft Publisher** (or any of them really), you upload your photo, position the author name on it – top or bottom, your choice. Position the title (centred? to the right? NOT on the left – too near the spine). Put the text in the spine [*try it – it just writes down instead of across.*]

(vii) Copy and paste your blurb about the book and about you, onto the *back cover* [this will be attention-grabbing and about 3-5 lines]. Next, if you've had people read it, some *one* line reviews, maybe a quote from the book?

(viii)   **DON'T** use fancy fonts, pale coloured text on a pale background or dark text on a dark background. Don't you find it annoying when people do this? What's important is that your title stands out and is readable, as is your name. Save it in **pdf** format.

Now back to **Amazon KDP**. You've already uploaded and saved your *Interior* file. Now click on *Cover*. Upload your *cover pdf*. Save. Now go to Pricing. Choose your selling price. It will convert it to Euros and dollars for you. Click Save. Now click Publish. Give it about 24 hours – they will get back to you and you'll see your book - page by page onscreen, you can turn the pages and review the layout (*exciting!*).

   Any problems they identify, go back to your original **Word** file and correct them. Same for the cover – go back to the original **jpeg** and revise that. Then load up **Amazon KDP** again, upload the revised *Interior* file or cover. Press *Publish* again. Bingo it's done.

   Order a sample book (if it's a print book) – cost around $5-6. It'll arrive within 2 weeks. Hold it in your hand. Hey you're a published

AUTHOR. How does it feel, all that work was worth it?

Check it carefully for typos, editing flaws and include the cover – how does it look? Do that before you make the 50-150 book order for the Book Launch. Upload the corrected file. Order your box of books. Yippee!

Chapter 19 Publicity & marketing

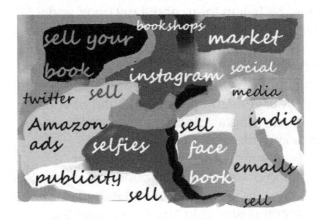

These days whether you are with a good publishing company or you're an Indie author, you must be involved in marketing. The days of authors saying 'Oh No, I'll just write the book', are over, unless you have oodles of money to spend on paying a publicist to do it for you or a contract with one of the Big Five companies.

I'm going to focus on Indie authors (Independent) first and give a brief guide to what you can do, but it's the same advice on the whole, even if you have a publisher – check with them.

You have to bite the bullet and stop trying to be modest. Start talking loudly about your book – now. For a British person this is particularly painful. We are taught the virtues of being self-effacing and NEVER shouting about our accomplishments. This is considered to be bragging, which is a complete No-No in British society.

I was absolutely horrified that I would be expected to 'sell' to my own circles of family and friends, by telling them about my book and highlighting the price. I swore I'd NEVER do that. But (sigh) now I'm more used to it. You don't bombard people, but it's OK if you remind them periodically about your book or tag a brief link to your Amazon page at the end of your emails and blog articles and ask them to share with their contacts.

For Americans perhaps it's easier, depending on family background of course. But generally Americans are taught to be proud of their accomplishments and shout them loud. For the rest of the world, you have variations between the two extremes.

Firstly there's ACTIVE and PASSIVE marketing. Let me explain.

Active marketing
Briefly this is marketing in which you take an active part
- arranging your book launch,
- doing talks in bookshops and local libraries,
- contacting media eg. local/ national newspapers, asking to do interviews,
- doing mail shots amongst friends and family and extended groups on social media.

Passive marketing
In short, for 'passive marketing', you create ongoing viewing of yourself and your books without having to constantly be 'doing' stuff.
- include links to your blog, links to the Amazon review page (below your book listing) plus Front

Matter on all your books as well as on the back page of your e-book/book.

- Creating and maintaining **your brand** as an author – for example having a regularly updated website/blog. Put up your author profile on Amazon at Author Central. Keep it up-to-date. Have you won a competition? Other publications? Short story in a magazine?
- Add a link after your signature on emails you send, leading to your website/blog. For example on Hotmail go to Settings/Signature, click and enter what you want – mine is like this

So that's author name, then email address, then

> Anna Meryt
>
> anna.meryt@ameryt.com
>
> **www.ameryt.com**
>
> (My Blog)
>
> @ameryt ....
> (Twitter)

website link address, then Twitter handle. You can put more of course – Instagram handle, Facebook name, LinkedIn name etc. Every email I send out ends with that 'signature'.

Marketing also comes in stages. There's pre-publication, publication and post-publication marketing.

Pre-publication

You market your book before publication, to create an interest in advance.

- post samples/extracts in advance, free tasters on your website – with a picture of your cover.

• Start looking for beta-readers, by that I mean people who you can offer to give your eBook to, for free, in exchange for a review on Amazon. Aim for at least twenty reviews on Amazon as soon as possible after book launch. This starts pushing you up the Amazon ranking list. Otherwise your book will sink without trace. Try literate friends, family and then Goodreads – who have many 'beta' readers (that's people willing to read your book, if you give it to them free, who regularly write reviews). What you want is reviews on Amazon, by Amazon-verified readers - they've got their book from Amazon.

• Contact local press. Please be aware that journalists can sound interested initially but then don't write about your book. You can try to badger them a bit. You have to have a publicity angle to grab their attention. Send them info, invite them to your book launch, make it sound interesting, up the drama. But unless you're a celeb or famous or notorious they may not come. If your book has an angle that is connected to your local area or local history, you might get their attention.

• Find blogs that review books and blogs that relate to your genre and contact them

• Look in Google Plus – find communities relating to your subject matter, find forums relating to your topic.

• Finally organise the time, date and venue of your book launch. Ask in a local independent bookshop if you can have it there. Or try local libraries and community centres. Then publicise it – do posters (A5 size is best) and put them up everywhere you can think of – libraries, community centres, bookshops, etc.

• Tell everyone on Facebook, Twitter, Instagram, Google Plus and any writer websites you belong to.

*   *   *

Publication

Before you upload your Interior Matter (your manuscript file) to Amazon KDP – in the back of the book, provide links to your website, Facebook page, Twitter name, Google Plus.

Write a '**Note from the Autho**r – be warm/friendly – ask readers for a review and tell them where to go to write it (on Amazon).

• **Amazon KDP** and **Kindle Direct Publishing** (**KDP**) both ask for *Keywords* when you've uploaded your book – *these are vital*. They match your subject matter to searches that people make on Google. You're allowed up to 7 keywords free on KDP.

Do some research – go to Google and search for other memoirs that are related to yours in some way, in subject area or country setting. Scroll down and check out what subject area headings and then sub- headings they come under.

I did this and found that memoirs similar (in time and place) to mine were in a category in Kindle eBooks titled Biography and True Accounts, then Historical, then Africa – so those were the key words to put in my KDP book upload. Another was under Ethnic and National –all these used up some of my Keywords in that KDP section. Another was under Autobiography and then Memoir. If your book is set in a particular, place, country – eg. South Africa, Manchester, Guadeloupe, Dubai whatever – make that one of your keywords. Perhaps choose a theme from your book eg. 'redemption', sailing, travel, political activism, spirituality…campaign groups etc. Search Amazon Kindle and Google and learn how they categorise their sections.

Now your book is uploaded, Amazon KDP have passed it, and you've chosen your price per book. Order one (or two) sample book(s), check it through carefully. See if there's more editing needed, if you need to tweak it a bit more – then re-upload the Word file/manuscript to Amazon KDP. If you plan to sell the majority of your books yourself and have several marketing events lined up, stock up by ordering about 50-150 from Amazon **several months** in advance (unless you're using a local **Print Shop**). For Amazon, you can order via Amazon KDP – where you've uploaded your interior matter and cover. They will charge you enough per book to cover their costs for printing and shipping/postage – it's relatively cheap – around £3-4 (($5-6) per book. This'll cost you about £150-£200. ($116-$155)

• Now you're all set. Time to plan how you want to do the book launch. Do you have public speaking skills? If the thought of speaking in public sends you into paralysis, do a short course before the event, to improve your skills. Practise at home, reading out the extracts you want to show off – to your partner, kids, even the cat. Prepare the room where you're going to sit/stand in advance. Keep lifting up your head and breathing, look to the back of the room, look at people's faces, not the ceiling. Speak clearly. Choose which extracts from your book you want to read out. If you are incredibly shy and public speaking induces a state of paralysis – get someone else to help out and support you, someone confident. You want to emphasise the drama and uniqueness of your story. Remember you want to make this event work. You want to sell your book.

*　*　*

Post-Publication Your book is now on Amazon and Kindle (Direct Publishing - KDP) or other eBook outlets like KOBO. The book launch has come and gone. How do you keep up the momentum? Years ago, when an author got published by a big publisher, they did lots of publicity, marketing and promoting of a book for about 3-6 months. Then it tailed off and finally sales would fade out and die. Shelf space in bookshops was needed for the next book on promotion. Nowadays, with Amazon and online book sales, a book can be promoted *ad infinitum*…. Sales can go on generating income for the author, if promoted to the right niche, indefinitely.

• On your website – use Mailchimp or Mailerlite to create an emailing list – Mailchimp is free if you have under 2000 contacts on your email list. Offer a Free Gift to your readers eg. a short story you've written or a chapter from this or another book of yours, to anyone who subscribes to your mailing list. Remember your readers are not fools, so make sure your gifts are genuine and reflect your best writing. You can do this before or after the launch.

• When you hit sales milestones – let your email list know eg. I've now sold 100 books, 500 books, 1000 books.

• Thank readers for reviews.

• Facebook Ads are another sales tool. You pay for these, but you choose how much you want to spend for example, $1 a day.

• There's loads of Twitter promos you can pay for too – but beware some may be scams. Do your research. Books Go Social does a Twitter promo that's popular. It's an effort to keep up the momentum. You have to just keep plugging on. It's particularly difficult if you've already started your next book project. You don't want to be distracted – 'I'm an author, not a salesperson', you cry. Well unless you have an amazing deal with a top publisher, who will organise a team of marketing and publicity people to launch your book (lucky you), tough cookies. You have to DO IT YOURSELF.

Chapter 20 Summing up ...

Sometimes extraordinary and interesting things happen to each of us. Often we feel strongly that these stories must be told. We can spend a lifetime talking about our story and how we're going to write a book one day. People may frequently say to you, '*You should write a book*', when you tell them some of your story.

To be a writer, to write and complete that story, you have to have passion and determination. As Maya Angelou stated in my quote at the beginning of this book

'There is no greater agony than bearing an untold story inside you.'

Many of our stories will die with us, untold. Don't be one of those who take their dramatic or interesting story to the grave. If you've got to this chapter reading this book, I feel sure you won't be one of those.

But it takes skill and absolute determination to write a memoir. You can't just pick up a pen and write (although that's a good way to start) without learning about description and character and voice and finding out how narrative works.

There are quite a few books I recommend to aspiring writers, to help you to build up the habit of writing. What's also important to do in this internet age is to read – read *books*. If you want to write a good memoir, read other memoir writers. Go to bookshops and look at the covers. Read the first page and see what grabs you, what makes you want to buy the book. Read good authors, read bad authors too if you like – compare them, become discerning, what makes this one so good and that one so bad. Which one is more enjoyable…. why?

Harry Bingham, a crime writer, gave a talk at a Literary Festival I went to a few years ago. Something he said stood out for me about what it's like for him to read other crime fiction – not his own obviously. He said that whenever he reads other authors now, because he's read and analysed so much crime writing, he can no longer become totally absorbed in the stories. Why? Because he's either admiring technique or recognising technique or criticising poor structure and technique.

Is this less of a problem for memoir writers? I don't think so. You still need to spot good structure, style and technique in a memoir, just as much as Harry Bingham reading crime fiction. But it doesn't spoil my enjoyment reading a true story.

Whatever kind of story telling you do, whether it is short stories, TV dramas, docu-dramas, history writing or fiction, you need to be good at your craft, make your characters interesting and tell a gripping, well-structured story. You need to bring the page to life and make your reader want to turn over the page to see what happens next.

Whatever writer you hear talk about their writing techniques (have a look on You Tube), they will all agree on one thing that will improve your writing – READ, READ, READ.

If you've got children, work full-time, maybe you have to fit in writing in an hour at night or in the early morning. You have to snatch bits of time where you can. I did all of that in a quite haphazard and unstructured way. Then finally finished my first book when I retired. Some people are much more organised than I was. But here I am with one memoir finished and published, and another in progress. Plus this book and another 'how to' book planned.

You think if you give up the day job and have all that time to write you'll be so much more productive? I have found that it's amazing what comes up to fill the space. Suddenly you're writing time shrinks rapidly. I'm an expert at prevarication … if I'm at home, the dishwasher needs emptying, I've run out of milk or I have to make lunch (what really, spend two hours at it?). So, I plan my day to leave the house at any time from 12-2 (there's Facebook, the laundry, phone calls and that cupboard must be cleaned ….).

I go to libraries or cafes, where none of those distractions exist … well except, I'll just check something on Facebook, answer that email, empty my Junk Mail…. whittle down my 'work' time with as many distractions as possible.

Think about where you like to write? At home or somewhere else? With total silence or the buzz of background conversation or with background music playing?

Time spent prevaricating is not always wasted. It's time spent building ideas, which are coagulating, expanding in the back of your brain. When you do finally start writing, the words can flow off your pen or keyboard.

I include therefore a list of books to read – all books that have helped me and countless other writers to get going and keep up with the writing. Books that have given me ideas, helped me structure my day, made me laugh and given me the courage to carry on.

THE END

Acknowledgements

So many people to thank for supporting the process of writing my book.

THANK YOU THANK YOU THANK YOU

- **Jam in a Jar** – my local bar/café for putting up with me writing for hours with a snack and a cappuccino. Quto for the music, the inspiring venue. Alberto for your support and enthusiasm.

- **Bettina Von Cossel** for agreeing to edit my manuscript at short notice. You edited in detail with invaluable commentary.

- **Alison Macdonald** my English friend in Morocco for being a great 'beta-reader' and giving me a whole page of feedback – ALL useful.

- **Edmund Coulthard**, my brother, a busy CEO of Blast Productions, for very useful comments – all good.

- To my daughters **Pascale** and **Tamlyn** who continue (as always) to encourage my writing and give invaluable feedback.

- All the interesting, fascinating, wannabe memoir writers who have attended my Memoir Writing courses – you inspired me to write this book – all of you.

- **Freya Newmarch** (and Charlie) for using their top-class artistic skills in helping design the book cover I wanted.

AND all the great memoir writers out there whose books I have read and who have inspired my small efforts.

Read on for extras …

My recommended bibliography

Title	Author	Year	Publisher
Writing the Memoir *(Highly recommended)*	Judith Barrington	1997	The 8th Mountain Press, USA
Arvon Book of Life Writing **(Essays**)) *[out of print]*	Sally Cline Carole Angier	2010	Methuen Drama GB
The Complete Artist's Way *Creativity as a Spiritual Practice*	Julia Cameron	2007	JP Tarcher
The Artist's Way Morning Pages **Journal**	Julia Cameron	2011	Souvenir Press
Writing down the Bones	Natalie Goldberg	1994	
Writing Your Way	Manjusvara	1986	Shambala Pubs
On Writing Well: The Informal **Guide to Writing Non-Fiction.**	William Zinser	1991	Longman Higher Education
Bird by Bird: Instructions on **Writing and Life – a classic.**	Anne Lamott	1980	Bantam Doubleday
He Stood, She Sat: *What your* *characters do while they talk.*	Ginger Hanson	2014	Saderra Publishing
She said He said - all about writing dialogue	Ginger Hanson	2019	Saderra Publishing
On Writing: A Memoir of the **Craft** *(Excellent)*	Stephen King	2012	Hodder paperbacks
The Sense of Style: **The Thinking Person's Guide to** **Writing in the 21st century.**	Steven Pinker	2015	Penguin
Writing Yourself: Transforming **PERSONAL Material**	J. Killick/ M Schneider	2010	Continuum Int. Pub. Grp.
The Creative Writing H/book	J. Singleton, M. Luckhurst	1999	Palgrave
The Pocket Book of **Proofreading**	William Critchley	1996	Macmillan Press
Eats Shoots and Leaves (sort out your apostrophes)	Lynne Truss	2011	Fourth Estate
Smashwords Book Marketing **Guide (Free on Kindle)**	Mark Coker	2011	Smashwords
The Smashwords Style Guide	Mark Coker	2014	
Secrets to Ebook Publishing **Success**	Mark Coker	2014	
Amazon KDP and Kindle Self- **Publishing Masterclass**	Rick Smith	2013	
To Self-Publish or Not to Self- **Publish**	Mick Rooney	2011	Troubadour Pub. Ltd

Here's a few websites to look at

- **Writers and Artists – how to find an agent**
  https://www.writersandartists.co.uk/writers/preparing-
  for-submission/how-to-find-a-literary-agent
- **Harry Bingham's website - www.agenthunter.co.uk**
  (excellent – has courses too) Now called **Jericho
  Writers**
- **Why Authors Walk Away from the Big Five**
  https://janefriedman.com/walk-away-good-big-5-
  publishers/
- **Advice for New Indie Authors from Self-Publishing
  Veterans**
  http://www.publishersweekly.com/pw/by-
  topic/authors/pw-select/article/64035-self-
  publishing-stars-speak-out.html
- **The Alliance of Independent Authors**

  https://www.allianceindependentauthors.org/

You could also take a look at:
- **Mark Dawson**'s marketing courses – find at
  www.indieauthor.com – expensive but worth it
  apparently. His 101 Course teaches you how to
  market your book on social media, there's Ads for
  Authors. Also look at his talks on YouTube (free).
- **An alternative is to pay someone professional to
  market your book …**
- The fastest way to create and self-publish your book –
  Lulu.com https://www.lulu.com/
- or look up the Amazon self-publishing platforms –**KDP
  – Kindle Direct Publishing www.kdp.amazon.com** –
  they have good support and instruction sections, and
  Kindle Create for formatting your manuscript for the
  Kindle e-reader..

You'll find plenty more. . .

.... and some blogs to follow

including mine – I write regular articles for
  writers.

- www.ameryt.com
- http://greenacrewriters.blogspot.co.uk/
- https://twodropsofink.com/
- http://www.dorkface.co.uk/
- lindsaybamfield.blogspot.com/
- emilybenet.blogspot.com/
- www.christopherfielden.com

My Top 20 Favourite Memoirs

As you will notice, I like memoirs set in Africa ... make a list of the best memoirs you've read. If you're going to write one, you need to look at style and technique in memoir writing. Don't just read the memoirs of the famous. What makes you pick up those by ordinary people like you and me?

	Title	Author	Publisher
1	The Shadow of the Sun	Ryzard Kapuscinsky	Penguin 2002
2	On Writing: a Memoir of the Craft	Stephen King	Hodder 2012
3	Conversations with God Book One	Neale Donald Walsch	Hodder & Stoughton 1997
4	Don't Let's Go to the Dogs Tonight	Alexandra Fuller	Picador 2002
5	Twenty Chicken's for a Saddle: A Story of an African Childhood	Robyn Scott	Penguin 2008
6	Long Walk to Freedom	Nelson Mandela	Abacus 1995
7	Dreams From My Father	Barack Obama	Canongate 2007
8	I Know Why The Caged Bird Sings	Maya Angelou	Virago 1984
9	Every Secret Thing	Gillian Slovo	Virago 2009
10	Is That It?	Bob Geldof	Sidgewiick &Jackson 1986
11	The Girl With Seven Names	Hyeonseo Lee	William Collins 2016
12	My Father's Places: A Memoir by Dylan Thomas' Daughter	Aeronwy Thomas	Skyhorse Pub. 2010
13	**Portrait of the Artist As A Young Dog/ A Child's Christmas in Wales**	Dylan Thomas	Guild Books 1948
14	Born a Crime: Stories from an African Childhood	Trevor Noah	John Murray 2017
15	A Street Cat Named Bob	James Bowen	Hodder 2016
16	Giving Up The Ghost: A Memoir	Hilary Mantel	Fourth Estate 2010
17	The Kon-Tiki Expedition	Thor Heyerdahl	Harper Collins 1982
18	The Elephant Whisperer	Lawrence Anthony	Sidgewick & Jackson 2009

If you seriously want to be an author you do need to have your own Facebook/Twitter / Instagram accounts and your own website/blog and keep updating it.

If you've found this book useful (or even if not) don't forget to leave a review on the Amazon website under the following book title:

Writing Memoir:
How to Write a Story from Your Life
by Anna Meryt.

Find the title and keep scrolling down until you get to reviews. Do give me a star rating (I really don't mind how many), I value your feedback in order to improve my book.

Write something even if there's only one line.

You can also take a look at my website –
www.ameryt.com. I try to make it a writer's resource by writing regular articles for writers (and readers) about how you can improve your writing. Also you'll find, on the right-hand side of my website (scroll down) a list of blogs by other authors and writers, who write interesting articles on blogging, writing and how to get published, self-publish and become an Indie author.

One more thing – perhaps you'd like to get on **my email list.** Don't worry, I won't bombard you. Maybe you'll get one a fortnight/month, with a story, an article, sometimes even a poem – something interesting or inspiring. I'm just setting up a mailing list you can access via my website, just drop me a line to **anna.meryt@ameryt.com**. Put 'Mailing List' in the subject line.

Warm wishes

Anna Meryt

www.ameryt.com

About the Author

Anna Meryt's first book – a memoir set in South Africa in the 1970s, where she had lived for a few years was published in 2015.
It's called
A Hippopotamus at The Table
(available on Amazon – as print or e-book)
Her second memoir
Beyond the Bounds
will be out in 2021.

She is also a prize-winning poet with several collections in print – '**Heart Broke**' and '**Dolly Mix**'.

Here's a taster from her next book **Beyond The Bounds**, set in London and Indonesia. This chapter won a *Highly Commended* prize in the Winchester Writers Festival 2017.

BEYOND THE BOUNDS

Chapter 1 A telephone call

I closed the front door behind me and walked up the stairs to the door of my flat. I was carrying two shopping bags and my work rucksack. The keys were in my mouth. I swapped the shopping to my left hand, my fingers cramping with the weight, took the key out of my mouth with my right hand, unlocked the door and kicked it open. I walked straight ahead into the kitchen, past the bathroom on my right. The kitchen was a good size for a London apartment, with bay windows overlooking a row of gardens down below. I dumped all the bags on the kitchen table. Phew! I glanced over at the phone in an alcove by the door. The red light was flashing. I remember the moment so well -- that red light signaled the beginning of a series of events that would change my life. We'll come back to that.

Made in the USA
Monee, IL
15 June 2021